Jaina Epistemology

Including the Jaina Theory of Error

JAYANDRA SONI

ADITYA PRAKASHAN
New Delhi

First Published, 2018

ISBN 978-81-934621-3-3

Published by Aditya Prakashan, 2/18, Ansari Road,
New Delhi – 110 002.

email: contact@adityaprakashan.com
website: www.adityaprakashan.com

Printed at Replika Press Pvt. Ltd.

Dedicated to the memories of Professors
M.D. Vasantharaj and N. Vasupal

About the author

Jayandra Soni retired in May 2012 from the Department of Indology and Tibetology, University of Marburg, Germany where he had taught Indian languages (Sanskrit, Hindi and Gujarati) and Indian philosophy from 1991–2012. Born and brought up in South Africa where he did his BA (University of Durban, Westville) in 1972, he studied further at the Banaras Hindu University, India (PhD 1978) and the McMaster University, Canada, for his second Phd (1987). He now lives in Innsbruck, Austria, continuing his own studies and teaching at the University of Innsbruck as a part-time lecturer. His publications can be seen here: http://www.staff.uni-marburg.de/~soni/.

Table of Contents

Preface

An attempt is being made to deal with the most significant aspects of Jaina epistemology as depicted in the separate chapters of this study. One aim is to try and demonstrate not only the complexity of the topic from the Jaina perspective but also to bring out the particular Jaina contribution to the subject: there are several aspects which evince the Jaina endeavour in contributing to the history of ideas in Indian thought. Suffice it to give one example here. In the history of Indian philosophy the favourite theme of *guṇa* and *guṇin* (a quality and the bearer of it) has been treated by the Jainas in their concern with *dravya*, *guṇa* and *paryāya* (a substance, its quality or qualities and the specific mode or modification of a particular object which serves as the manifestation of the substance). That these concepts, and particularly the term *paryāya*, have significant epistemological implications has not been sufficiently brought out, if at all, in the available literature on Jaina epistemology.

With their view on *paryāya*, that is the specific mode which allows a substance to take because of its particular qualities, the Jainas have uniquely applied the idea consistently to both their *jīva* and *ajīva dravyas* or substances. These two *dravyas* constitute basic Jaina ontology and the relation between the two forms the basis of Jaina metaphysics. Epistemologically they constitute the subject as the knower and object to be known (*prameya*), as the chapter on *dravya*, *guṇa* and *paryāya* aims to bring out.

Similar is the case with the term *upayoga*. Its relevance not only for basic Jaina epistemology but also for the Jaina theory of error (*khyāti-vāda*) has rarely, if at all, been highlighted. Indian theories of knowledge or cognition usually give an account not only of so-called valid cognitions, but they also say that error that can occur in our cognition. Indian epistemologists and theoreticians usually strive to account for how error can occur in order, indeed, to bring out the 'validity' of cognition through various means, such as perception. The Jainas too contributed significantly to this debate with their cogitations on *upayoga* to account for both valid cognition and the possibility of the occurrence of error in our cognition.

This study of Jaina epistemology and its theory of error emerged gradually in so far as it was only later discovered that the various aspects of the theme, separated here in different chapters, in fact belong together. In my studies in Jaina philosophy I began with first attempting to understand Jaina ontology and metaphysics which led me to the ramifications of *dravya*, *guṇa* and *paryāya*, which was then published in 1991. This was followed by further research published in 2007, 2012 and 2015, culminating in this study which now brings together the main points of the topic. The merit, if any, in bringing them together again here is to bring out their evident inter-relatedness as a single unit. There are other aspects that can also be easily related to Jaina epistemology, like the theory of manifoldness (*anekānta-vāda*) and the role of the cognition/knowledge concealing (*āvaraṇīya*) karmas. These aspects will only be hinted at.

Jayandra Soni
Innsbruck, Austria
October 2017

Chapter 1
Introduction: Epistemology Matters

One of the earliest and intensive occupations with epistemological matters was done by the renowned Sāṅkhya teacher Vṛṣagaṇa (Vārṣagaṇa or Vārṣagaṇya, perhaps 300 CE). He is considered to be the first thinker who investigated epistemological questions at the beginning of his work, the *Ṣaṣṭitantra* (available only in fragments), and thereby began a tradition followed by others.[1]

The development of Indian epistemology clearly goes hand in hand with the development of debate in India. The emergence of philosophical debate in India is clearly traceable not only in the form of organized public contests since early times, but also in the commentary literature to the basic works of each school where it was employed in a refined style. This activity contributed greatly to a sharpening of the philosophical tools and to the setting down of rules of debate which had to be strictly adhered to in the courts where the debates usually took place, and also in the form of arguments in scholastic debates.

That the theory of knowledge has been a favourite topic from very early times is also evident from a work on Indian medicine, perhaps in the first century of our era, but the ideas in it were most probably in vogue even earlier. The work was compiled by Caraka in his now famous *Caraka-saṃhitā* (CS). The author (in CS 3, 8) advises medical practitioners to debate with others because discussion increases the zeal for knowledge,

---

[1] See Frauwallner 1958, Ruegg 1962 and Obhammer 1960.

clarifies knowledge, increases the power of speech, makes one famous, removes doubt and establishes the knowledge already gained. Moreover, one can learn new things in a discussion, especially when carried away with the zeal of the discussions, the other person discloses information which would otherwise be kept secret. In this very early period in the history of Indian debate it was also recognized that a discussion, which forms the basis of a debate can be of different kinds. Caraka distinguishes two kinds, one that is "friendly" and one that is "hostile".[2] Caraka's list contains 44 items which the physician should have a command over before accepting an invitation to enter into a debate. The list is being supplied entirely because it is interesting to note them in full here for the terms that were, and continued to be, significant for epistemology and Indian philosophy generally. Moreover, its influence on the Nyāya school is also noteworthy, which succinctly used the list in a more refined manner, for example, including all the epistemological terms under one, single category, as will be shown below. The Nyāya school has to be mentioned because of its impact on the development of logic and epistemology. Even a fleeting glance at Caraka's list evinces the significance the terms had at that time and for the enduring relevance they have retained, especially for epistemological matters. Caraka's list of the 44 terms is:

1. dispute (*vāda*), 2. substance (*dravya*), 3. quality (*guṇa*), 4. movement (*karma*), 5. generality (*sāmānya*), 6. particularity (*viśeṣa*), 7. inherence (*samavāya*), 8. thesis (*pratijñā*), 9. statement of the proof for the thesis put forward (*sthāpanā*), 10. the opposite statement of the opponent (*pratiṣṭhāpanā*), 11.

---

[2] For a detailed description of the various kinds of debate and the different kinds of assemblies which decide the outcome of the debate, see Dasgupta 1953, pp. 378–388 and Frauwallner 1994, p. 66. Useful in this context is also Obherhammer 1963, pp. 63–103. See also Soni 2000, on which this part is based.

reason (*hetu*), 12. application (*upanaya*), 13. conclusion (*nigamana*), 14. rejoinder (*uttara*), 15. example (*dṛṣṭānta*), 16. tenet (*siddhānta*), 17. communication (*śabda*), 18. perception (*pratyakṣa*), 19. inference (*anumāna*), 20. tradition (*aitihya*), 21. comparison (*aupamya*), 22. doubt (*samśaya*), 23. the purpose one follows (*prayojana*), 24. going astray (*savyabhicāra*), 25. inquiry or desire to know (*jijñāsā*), 26. ascertainment (*vyavasāya*), 27. presumption (*arthaprāpti*), 28. the origin as a means to infer the beginning (*sambhava*), 29. the questionable (*anuyojya*), 30. the unquestionable (*ananuyojya*), 31. the question (*anuyoga*), 32. the counter-question (*pratyanuyoga*), 33. defect of speech (*vākyadoṣa*), 34. excellence of speech (*vākpraśaṃsā*), 35. quibble (*chala*), 36. fallacy (*ahetu*), 37. lapse of the right time (*atītakāla*), 38. objection (*upālambha*), 39. rejection of the objection (*parihāra*), 40. abandonment of the thesis (*pratijñāhāni*), 41. admission of the opposite thesis (*abhyanujñā*),[3] 42. incorrect reason (*hetvantara*), 43. missing the point (*arthāntara*), and 44. reasons for defeat (*nigrahasthāna*).

The Nyāya school efficiently used this list, making it compact and using it as the foundation of its entire system. Its favourite topic was epistemology. The very first *sūtra* of the *Nyāya-sūtra*, with its 16 terms can be seen as a summary of Caraka's categories. A knowledge of these 16 terms is said to lead to the highest good (*niḥśreyasa*) and forms the starting point for all the themes Nyāya deals with in its basic work. The 16 terms listed at the very beginning of the *Nyāya-sūtra* (1, 1) are interesting to note here to show their relation to the emergence of philosophical debate in India and for their special emphasis on epistemological issues. Moreover, most schools adopted the formal presentation of an argument from

[3] In his footnote to this Frauwallner p. 70 notes: "A recognition of what the opponent says is also the important point included here, when one says: 'You commit the same mistake', since one acknowledges the justification of the rebuke."

the Nyāya model. The 16 basic categories in the Nyāya system are: 1. the instruments or means of knowledge (*pramāṇa*), 2. the object of knowledge (*prameya*), 3. doubt (*saṃśaya*), 4. purpose (*prayojana*), 5. example (*dṛṣṭānta*), 6. tenet (*siddhānta*), 7. members of the argument (*avayava*), 8. deliberation (*tarka*), 9. conclusion (*nirṇaya*), 10. disputation (*vāda*), 11. debate (*jalpa*), 12. wrangling (*vitaṇḍā*), 13. fallacious reasons (*hetvābhāsa*), 14. quibble (*chala*), 15. false objections (*jāti*) and 16. reasons for defeat (*nigrahasthāna*).

Each school accepted a fixed number of instruments or means of cognition (*pramāṇa*), each of which yields a particular kind of knowledge, and for the major schools of Indian philosophy the number ranges from one to six. So, for example, the materialist accepts only perception as the most important and reliable means of knowledge, the Buddhists and the Vaiśeṣika school accept inference as well, the Sāṅkhya school accepts authoritative verbal testimony (*āpta-vacana*) in addition to perception and inference, etc.

There are certain implicit conditions on the basis of which the number of means of cognition were accepted by each school. At least four conditions need to be fulfilled for a particular means of cognition to retain its particular validity: (a) the knowledge which one means of cognition furnishes must be *new* and not attainable by any other means; (b) one means of cognition may aid another in making a particular knowledge possible but the means of cognition in question should *not be reducible to another*—so, e.g., when perception aids inference, as in inferring fire by seeing the smoke in the distance, the knowledge gained cannot be reduced to the knowledge obtained by perception alone; (c) the cognition obtained through one particular means of knowledge should not be contradicted by another means of knowledge; (d) the accepted means of cognition should *appeal to reason* and in the case of verbal testimony or scriptural authority, for example, the knowledge concerning the revealed truth must appear *probable* and be made intelligible in terms of human experience, otherwise such a means of cognition may be said to fail in its purpose. It is clear that these conditions also apply to the Jaina theory of knowledge.

In the history of Indian epistemology two approaches emerged with reference to the specific means of cognition and how exactly they can be regarded as valid means. These are *svataḥ-prāmāṇya-vāda* and *parataḥ-prāmāṇya-vāda*.

Svataḥ-prāmāṇya-vāda is the theory of intrinsic validity of cognition as accepted by the Mīmāṃsakas, Vedāntins, Śaiva Siddhāntins and the Jainas: for them valid cognition, namely empirical knowledge, is true by its very nature and the so-called erroneous nature of cognition or invalidity of knowledge is due to some defect in the means or source of cognition (*kāraṇa-doṣa*), like defective eyesight, or as the Jainas say, due to the obscuring karmas (*āvaraṇīya-karma*). Thus, one cannot a priori speak of 'false knowledge' but rather of an error in the means through which cognition takes place, either through a defect in the organ of perception or through the negative effect of karma. This view of intrinsic validity of cognition is opposed to:

Parataḥ-prāmāṇya-vāda, the theory of extrinsic validity of cognition propounded preeminently by the Nyāya and Vaiśeṣika schools. For them an extraneous factor or condition needs to be fulfilled in the origin (*utpatti*) or ascertainment (*jñapti* also *jñāpti*) of cognition to establish its validity. The question for them is not how knowledge comes to be true or false, but rather how we become aware of its truth or falsity. For this we require fruitful activity (*saṃvādi-pravṛtti*) as an additional condition, namely its appeal to facts. Thus for Nyāya all knowledge is either true or false, there being no 'neutral' knowledge — doubt is a kind of knowledge that one has, the truth or falsity of which is not yet seen.

The players in the epistemological process, *prāmāṇya-vāda*, are the following: the object to be cognised *(prameya)*, the subject that cognises (*pramātṛ*), the means (*pramāṇa*) through which the object is cognised, such as perception, thereby yielding the (valid) cognition (*pramā/pramiti*) of the object.

In other words, most Indian schools implicitly presuppose that when we cognise something, we can be basically certain of its validity. However, Indian thinkers have always acknowledged the fact that human cognition can be erroneous. That is, a comprehensive theory of cognition should not only explain how what we cognise can be regarded as valid, but such a theory should also be in a position to explain how erroneous cognition can take place, namely, to account for the possibility of its occurrence by taking into account the generally accepted possibility of human fallibility.

Indian theories of error (*khyāti-vāda*)

It may said that the soundness or success of a theory of valid cognition is commensurate with the success with which it 'explains' the occurrence of error. The question to which an answer was sought is: how does the occurrence of error fit into the structure of the human process of cognition? The question is significant because for the *ātmavādins*, for example, the self, or the *ātman*, intrinsically possesses knowledge — this would apply to Jaina philosophy as well insofar as, in this context, *jīva* can be seen as a synonym of the *ātman*. It is this point which has led Indian thinkers to propound several theories of error (*khyāti-vāda*) to try and account for how error creeps into the fabric of cognition. These can be broadly divided into so-called 'realistic' and 'idealistic' theories.[4]

[4] See Hiriyanna 1975, especially pp. 49–113, from which the points here have been drawn. See also Soni 1989, p. 165, note 114.

The 'realistic' theories of error are *akhyāti-vāda* and *anyathākhyātivāda*. *Akhyātivāda* is the theory that error in our cognition implies a lack of knowledge, namely, that error is partial or incomplete knowledge. In other words, there is in fact no error as such and one should speak, rather, of a failure to distinguish the positive features of an object of cognition from the negative ones. The criterion for deciding finally, is the applicability of the cognition or knowledge to practical life (*vyavahāra*). This theory of error is mainly associated with the Prābhākara school of Mīmāṃsā and, with significant variations, also with the Sāṅkhya school and the Viśiṣṭādvaita propounded chiefly by Rāmānuja (his version of the theory of error is also called *yathārtha-khyāti* or *sat-khyāti*).

The second 'realistic' theory of error is *anyathākhyāti-vāda*, the theory that error is the cognition of an object as 'otherwise', namely as other than what it in fact is. The theory is also called *viparīta-khyāti* or cognition that is 'reversed', i.e. reverse apprehension. This theory is advocated by the Bhāṭṭa school of Mīmāṃsā and the Nyāya-Vaiśeṣika, Yoga, Śaiva Siddhānta schools. The Jaina theory also belongs to this group of the realistic theories of error, the details of which will be shown later in this study.

There are three 'idealistic' theories of error in Indian thought. These are 1. *ātma-khyāti-vāda*, 2. *asat-khyāti-vāda* and 3. *anirvacanīya-khyāti-vāda*. 1. *Ātma-khyāti-vāda* is the theory of error that all experience in its objectivised mode is as such illusory and, by extension, the 'error' that can occur in cognition in everyday life is a 'double error'. This theory is advocated chiefly by the Yogācāra or Vijñāna-vāda school of Buddhism, and to a certain extent also Advaita Vedānta. 2. *Asat-khyāti-vāda* is the theory of error that error is the cognition of something that does not in fact exist. It is advocated with significant differences in its interpretation by the Madhyamaka school of Buddhism and the Madhva school of Vedānta. 3. *Anirvacanīya-khyāti-vāda* is the theory of error which points to an object that cannot be said to be this or that thing, i.e. the object is indeterminable. It means that "error points to a thing that is precisely like what it appears, but is yet not characterisable as either *is* or *is not* (*sad-asad-anirvacanīya*)".[5] Śaṅkara is the chief advocate of this theory of error.

The Indian theories of error make it evident that ultimately epistemological matters are closely linked with the metaphysics and ontology of the school concerned, especially because of the principal role of the subject who cognises (*pramātṛ*). The question how error creeps into our cognition rests upon a description, indeed a definition, of what constitutes the intrinsic nature of this subject that cognises a specific object and whose intrinsic nature also had to be defined to bring out the contrast between both the subject and object of cognition. In this sense, epistemology which primarily concerns cognition as a fact of our everyday world also points at the essential nature of the individual involved in the cognition process. In other words, the attention paid to epistemology as such served not only the purpose to provide a basis for an intelligible discourse on matters of common, everyday experience but also, even if indirectly, of distinguishing it from what constitutes the knowledge of ultimate reality, or of indicating how it could yield a knowledge of one's own essential nature, namely of the subject who cognises, as part of this ultimate reality. In the case of Jainism the conscious principle, called *jīva*, is one of two substances that make up reality (the other being the five insentient categories, collectively called *ajīva*). This means that correct cognition incorporates a knowledge of the natures of both substances, namely knowing the essential natures *jīva* and *ajīva*. How the Jainas explain this should be made explicit in the course of this study.

---

[5] See Hiriyanna 1975, p. 105.

Plan of this study

In the light of what has been already said, the basic point of Jaina epistemology concerns the immaterial world that is cognised, through the animated means of cognition such as perception, and also the conscious, sentient principle which is said to cognise and to make make cognition at all possible. As just pointed out, this involves in the case of Jainism a study of the natures of the conscious principle, called *jīva*, and of the five insentient categories, collectively called *ajīva*. Both are said to be substances or *dravya.*[6] However, to say that they are substances is made much more complex by the assertion that a substance is not conceivable without the particular form it takes on, because of the qualities which allow it to do so. Hence, we have in Jainism a threefold structure that applies to both the sentient and insentient substances: *dravya*, *guṇa* and *paryāya*, or the substance (*jīva-* or *ajīva-dravya*), the qualities (*guṇas*) that they possess which allow them to change or take on a specific mode (*paryāya*); for example, during cognition as will be shown in the case of the sentient principle, or clay into a pot for an insentient substance. In the case of the epistemological process the *paryāya* of *jīva,* the specific mode it takes on in the process, is crucial and the crux of Jaina epistemology. If one knows that this *paryāya* of *jīva* can be seen in the epistemological context as being identical to the term *upayoga*, the so-called function, application or faculty of the sentient principle, then with its unique function in the process of cognition, the link is evident between it and the mode which the qualities of the sentient principle 'allows' it to take on. The complexities of these themes will be elaborated in the chapters concerning *dravya*, *guṇa*, *paryāya*: their epistemological relevance (chapter 2) and *upayoga*: its unique function for cognition and knowledge (chapter 3). It is only the function of

[6] This statement is a summary of what is stated in TS 5, 1–3 and 39/38.

upayoga that evinces the possibility of error in the epistemological process. The Jaina *khyāti-vāda* or the theory of error will then be discussed in chapter 4.

As already pointed out, my study of Jaina epistemology and its theory of error emerged gradually in so far as it was discovered that the various aspects of the theme, separated here in different chapters, in fact belong together. In my studies in Jaina philosophy I began with first attempting to understand Jaina ontology and metaphysics which led me to the ramifications of *dravya*, *guṇa* and *paryāya*, which was then published in 1991. This was followed by further research published in 2007, 2012 and 2015, culminating in this study which now conveniently brings together the main points on the topic. There are other aspects that can also be easily related to Jaina epistemology, like the theory of manifoldness (*anekānta-vāda*) and the role of the cognition or knowledge-concealing (*āvaraṇīya*) karmas. These aspects will only be hinted at because they are better known, for example Matilal 1981, Jaini 1998 and Wiley 2004.

The reader's indulgence is craved for the inevitable repetitions in the different chapters. These were unavoidable because the studies in each chapter were gradually expanded and at each time the context had to be made clear.

Chapter 2
Dravya, *Guṇa* and *Paryāya* Their Epistemological Relevance

The main contents of this chapter were published in 1991.[1] At that time the direct epistemological relevance of these categories, which are crucial for basic Jaina philosophy as a whole, were not clearly worked out. The terms are generally translated as substance (*dravya*), quality (*guṇa*) and the mode or modification (*paryāya*) which a substance undergoes or takes on, because of the qualities inherent in it that allow it to do so, like gold being transformed into the various objects like a bangle, ring, etc., through the inherent qualities which allow such a modification. It is known that in Jainism there are two substances, *jīva* and *ajīva*, the principles of sentience and non-sentience. *Tattvārtha*-sūtra (TS) 5, 1–3 explicitly state that both *ajīva* and *jīva* are substances (*dravya*).[2] However, there is an added aspect to the concept of a *dravya*, namely that as a substance it possesses a quality or qualities and takes on a specific mode or modification, namely that the abstract category substance is in fact only cognisable through the particular mode it takes on, like a bangle or ring.

---

[1] It was published as "*Dravya, Guṇa* and *Paryāya* in Jaina Thought" in the *Journal of Indian Philosophy*, Netherlands: Kluwer, Vol. 19, 1991 pp. 75–88. I thank the Springer "Copyright Clearance Center" for kindly allowing me to reuse the article, email dated 6 October 2016.

[2] TS 5, 1–3 say: *ajīva-kāyā dharmādharmākāśa-pudgalāḥ / dravyāṇi / jīvāś ca*: 'the *ajīva* bodies (here categories) *dharma, adharma, ākāśa* and *pudgala* / are *dravyas* / the *jīvas* as well (are *dravyas*). TS 5, 39 mentions *kāla* separately as a *dravya*. TS 5, 38/37 says *guṇa-paryāyavad dravyam*, "that which posses *guṇa* and *paryāya* is a substance" (tr. Tatia 1994).

The story of the substances *ajīva* and *jīva* entails the stipulation (TS 5, 38/37) that both of them possess qualities and modes. These are easily understandable in the case of material (*ajīva*) objects, but the consistent application of these qualities and modes to the *jīva-dravya* as well, is what enables the link to their epistemological significance. This link is enabled because as will be seen below, it is the mode, the *paryāya* (called *upayoga* in the epistemological context), of the *jīva* that fulfils the epistemological function through the function, application or faculty of sentience, namely through its *upayoga*. In other words, in order to specifically grasp the notion of *upayoga*, it is necessary to see exactly what the Jainas say about *dravya, guṇa* and *paryāya* with reference to both the *jīva* and *ajīva* substances.

The philosophical significance of the terms *dravya, guṇa* and *paryāya*, a substance, its qualities and the mode or modification it undergoes or can undergo, is evidently to account for changes in both the *jīva* and *ajīva* substances, without the substances losing their substance-ness, their *dravyatva*, in any way, just as the gold ring retains its gold-ness and can be transformed into another golden object. The *jīva*-substance, like the other *ajīva*-substances, also undergoes changes, namely through *darśana* and *jñāna* that occur in it, referred together by the term *upayoga* (TS 2, 9). These are functions, applications or faculties of sentience (*cit* or *caitanya*) and *upayoga* is an inherent 'characteristic' (*lakṣaṇa*, TS 2, 8) of the *jīva-dravya*, without losing in any way its sentience or *jīvatva*. The reference to *darśana* and *jñāna* is what entails the direct relevance to epistemology, i.e. through *upayoga*, which in turn has to be understood in the context of *dravya, guṇa* and *paryāya*.

The specifics of *upayoga* are the content of the next chapter. This chapter first attempts to present the basics and the relevance of the concepts of substances, qualities and modes in Jaina philosophy not only generally, but also specifically, to show how out of them their epistemological significance can be extracted.

One of the clear presentations of substances, qualities and their modes is given by Kundakunda, whose dates unfortunately vary considerably from between the 2nd to the 8th centuries (see Dundas 2002, p. 107). If there were certainty about his dates, many ideas and their historical significance and development could have been clearer. Nonetheless, four philosophical masterpieces are ascribed to him (listed in the literature), among then the *Pravacana-sāra (Pavayaṇa-sāra)*, the 'Essence of Scripture' (PrS). This text has chiefly been chosen for its lucidity in dealing with the topic. Fortunately, the basics regarding the topic apply to Jaina philosophy as a whole and may be used as a basis for the perceptive ideas contained in them, and may also be seen as one of the specific contributions of the Jainas to the history of ideas in Indian philosophical activity as a whole.

It is generally agreed that the introduction of the term *guṇa* (quality) is relatively later than the terms *dravya* (substance) and *paryāya* (mode or modification) when philosophically discussing the state in which a *dravya* is in a particular moment of its existence.[3] *Paryāya* seems to have been used loosely and in a broad sense to include what later was distin-

[3] This is generally true even though perhaps the first canonical reference to these terms is in *Uttarādhyayanasūtra* 28, 5–6 (reference from Upadhye 1984, Introduction: *Śrī Kundakundācārya's Pravacana-sāra*, p. 65). These *sūtras* state the following: "... The wise ones have taught the knowledge of substances, qualities and all the developments. Substance is the substrate of qualities; the qualities are inherent in one substance; but the characteristic of developments is that they inhere in either (viz. substance or qualities)", Jacobi 1895, p. 153. The first footnote on the page clearly indicates that "substances, qualities and all developments" refer to *dravya, guṇa* and *paryāya* respectively.

guished as the *guṇa* of a thing.[4] When and why exactly the term *guṇa* was specifically introduced is difficult to assess conclusively but there is no doubt that the term was clearly distinguished from *paryāya* at least by the time of Kundakunda and Umāsvāti[5] who specifically deal with all three terms in their works. One suggestion, however, is that this "seems to be a later innovation due to the influence which the philosophy and terminology of Nyāya-Vaiśeṣika gradually gained over the scientific thoughts of the Hindus"[6] and another that it "must have come about from the spontaneous perception of an obvious gap in the ontological picture of a *dravya*".[7] The following observation is also noteworthy in this context:

> *Guṇas* are a quite usual feature of the Vaiśeṣika system; the notion of *paryāya* is peculiarly Jaina, though seen in its popular sense in later Nyāya works. In early Jaina works, like those of Kundakunda... the notion of *guṇas* is very simple; *guṇas* stand ... for the essential differentia of a thing; but in many later works the doctrine has been much more elaborated, possibly after the manner of the Vaiśeṣika system.[8]

Although the real reason for the use of the term *guṇa* may be a matter of speculation, it is nonetheless quite likely that its introduction is due to both the reasons given above, viz., for the purposes of philosophical detail and clarification, as well due to the influence of Nyāya-Vaiśeṣika terminology in the

---

[4] C.f: "... postulating the distinct category of *guṇa* must have been done ... posterior.., to the period when *paryāya* alone was accepted as the more inclusive category". Padmarajiah 1963, p. 260, in the footnote continued from the previous page.

[5] After surveying at length various opinions of scholars, Upadhye 1984, p. 21 believes that Kundakunda's age "lies at the beginning of the Christian era". Umāsvāti's dates are considered to be c. 3rd–4th centuries AD. See also K. K. Dixit's historical evaluation in Dixit 1974, p. 1, and the historical introduction by Chakravartinayanar in Kundakunda *Pañcāstikāya* 1975 ed., pp. i–xiii.

[6] Jacobi's introduction to *Jaina Sūtras*, p. xxxiv, see Jacobi 1895.

[7] Padmarajiah 1963, p. 260, in the fn.

[8] Upadhye 1984, introduction to *Pravacana-sāra*, p. 63.

context of Indian thought as a whole. A treatment of the categories of *dravya, guṇa* and *paryāya* as they are used in selected texts will be attempted here in order to see how the Jaina tradition, and particularly Kundakunda, dealt with them.

Kundakunda's starting point in the discussion on *dravya, guṇa* and *paryāya* may be said to be related to the question concerning what constitutes the objects of knowledge, which is the subject matter of the second chapter of his *Pravacanasāra* entitled *jñeya-tattvādhikāra.* In introducing this topic the commentator Amṛtacandra says that Kundakunda "properly explains in it the essential nature of *dravya, guṇa* and *paryāya* of a *padārtha*".[9] In common Jaina parlance *padārtha* is a synonym for *tattva* and refers to the seven basic truths or fundamental verities which form the basis of Jaina metaphysics.[10]

---

[9] *Atha jñeyatattva-prajñāpanaṃ tatra padārthasya samyag-dravya-guṇa-paryāya-svarūpam upavarṇayati*. A.N. Upadhye 1984, p. 107. The work is described as a pro-canonical text of the Jainas and this book contains a critical edition of the Prakrit text (translated into English by Upadhye, pp. 384–410) with the Sanskrit commentaries of Amṛtacandra (whose Sanskrit translation of the original Prakrit *gāthās* are cited in the paper) and Jayasena, and the Hindi commentary of Pāṇḍe Hemarāja. Unless otherwise stated the translations of the *gāthās* are Upadhye's.

[10] Umāsvāti enumerates the seven basic *tattvas* in his TS, I, 4: *jīva-ajīva-āsrava-bandha-saṃvara-nirjarā-mokṣās tattvam*. *Karman* is a key factor in understanding the sequence of these basic truths of Jaina metaphysics. Through the interaction between *jīva* and *ajīva*, which is said to have taken place since beginningless time, an aspect of *ajīva* (viz., *pudgala*) becomes converted into *karman* and clings to the *jīva*. This fact, as the Jainas see it, is realistically depicted as dust particles settling on an oiled surface. The effect of *karman* attaching itself or streaming (*āsrava*) into *jīva* restricts its powers of expression, characterised by the manifestation of consciousness intrinsic to its nature. Thus *jīva* is under bondage (*bandha*). It is, however, possible for *jīva* to prevent the inflow of *karman* through ascetic practices and this truth is expressed in the word *saṃvara*. Asceticism also helps *jīva* to rid itself of or burn away the *karman* that is already binding it and this truth is *nirjarā*. The effect of cleansing itself of all *karman* brings with it the *jīva's* liberation from the influence of *karman*, and this truth, which is the goal to be reached, is *mokṣa*.

Only the first two *tattvas* are also called *dravyas*, namely entities or substances that exist eternally and maintain throughout their *dravyatva* (substantiality). In the very first *gāthā* of this section Kundakunda introduces the theme which makes up the subject matter of most of the section. His statement is quite clearly made: *arthaḥ khalu dravyamayo dravyāṇi gunātmakāni bhaṇitāni / tais tu punaḥ paryāyāḥ* .... (*Pravacana-sāra*, PrS, II, 1: "The object of knowledge is made up of substances, which are said to be characterised by qualities, and with which, moreover, are (associated) the modifications..."

Thus it is clear that Kundakunda recognizes the categories *dravya*, *guṇa* and *paryāya*. By way of giving a definition of *dravya* he says:

> *aparityakta-svabhāvenotpāda-vyaya-dhruvatva-saṃyuktam* |
> *guṇa-vacca sa-paryāyarṃ yat tad dravyam iti bruvanti* || PrS II, 3.
>
> That is called a substance which is endowed with qualities and accompanied by modifications and which is coupled with origination, destruction and permanence without leaving its nature (of existence).[11]

This *gāthā* is a summary statement of three characteristics of a *dravya*, namely, that it is inextricably associated with *guṇa* and *paryāya*, that it retains its *dravyatva* despite the changes it

---

[11] The *gāthā* following this reiterates the point with the added statement emphasizing the existence of a *dravya* and leaves no doubt as to Kundakunda's standpoint regarding his acceptance of the three categories: *sad-bhāvo hi svabhāvo guṇaiḥ saha paryāyaiś citraiḥ* | *dravyasya sarva-kālam-utpāda-vyaya-dhruvatvaiḥ* || PrS II, 4, 'The nature of the substance is existence accompanied by qualities by its variegated modifications and by origination, destruction and permanence for all time'. Cf. also Kundakunda's *Pañcāstistikāya* 10: *dravyaṃ sal-lakṣaṇakam utpāda-vyaya-dhruvatva-saṃyuktam* | *guṇa-paryāya-āśrayaṃ vā yat-tad-bhaṇanti sarvajñāḥ* || 'The wise ones call a *dravya* what has the attribute of existence, is accompanied by origination, destruction and permanence, or is the locus of *guṇa* and *paryāya*. Kundakunda: *Pañcāstikāyaḥ*, 1983 ed., p. 24. The book contains the original Prakrit text with the Sanskrit commentaries by Amṛtacandra (whose Sanskrit translation of the text is used here) and Jayasena, and the Hindi commentary by Pāṇḍe Hemarāja.

apparently undergoes and, thereby, that it is existent or that it exists. The inseparability of these three terms is explicitly stated in PrS II, 18: *nāsti guṇa iti vā kaścit paryāya itīha yā vinā dravyam:* "There is nothing as a quality nor as a modification in the absence of a substance". That they are nonetheless distinct aspects is clearly asserted when Kundakunda says (II, 16):

> *yad dravyaṃ tan na guno yo'pi guṇah, sa na tattvam arthāt* |
> *eṣa hy atad-bhāvo naiva abhāva iti nirdiṣṭaḥ* ||
>
> Really speaking what is substance is not quality, nor what is quality is not substance; this is a case of non-identity and not of absolute negation.

Although *paryāya* is not mentioned here specifically, it may be assumed that it is also a distinct aspect that applies in the context under discussion here. It is significant to note also that the distinctness of the terms does not imply that they are exclusive of each other; hence one can speak of them as being inseparable.

The fundamental category that is the basis of the discussion at hand is *dravya* and what this category entails is stated in PrS II, 35:

> *dravyaṃ jīvo'jīvo jīvaḥ punaś cetanopayoga-mayaḥ* |
> *pudgala-dravya-pramukho'cetano bhavati ca-ajīvaḥ* ||
>
> Substance comprises Jīva, the sentient principle, and Ajīva, the non-sentient principle; Jīva is constituted of sentiency and manifestation of consciousness; Ajīva is insentient, and the foremost of this class is matter.[12]

The classification of *dravya* into two kinds, *jīva* and *ajīva*, is a basic tenet of Jaina ontology. Moreover, *ajīva* is a general

---

[12] The term *cetanopayoga* is translated as "manifestation of consciousness" by Upadhye. *Upayoga* is a technical term in Jainism and is perhaps better translated as "operation". Two such operations intrinsic to the nature of consciousness, which in fact signify its manifestation, are *jñāna* and *darśana*. Cf. Introduction by Jaini 1978 to Amṛtacandrasūri's *Laghu-tattva-sphoṭa*, p. 18. In his *Tattvārthasūtra* II, 8 Umāsvāti says with reference to *jīva-dravya*: *upayogo lakṣaṇam*, the operation or manifestation [of consciousness] is its characteristic mark. See also the next chapter below.

term under which five further *dravyas* are referred to: *pudgala, dharma, adharma, ākāśa* and *kāla.* Since *jīva* is the only sentient principle among the *dravyas*, it alone can 'know' the others. Kundakunda specifically mentions *pudgala* as the foremost among the *ajīva-dravyas*, indicating perhaps that it deserves to be noted in connection with *guṇa* and *paryāya.* In any case, *pudgala-dravya* features as one of the most important ontological categories insofar as it is *pudgala* that becomes transformed into *karman* which hinders, restricts or distorts the manifestation or operation (*upayoga*) of consciousness intrinsic to the nature of *jīva.* One can ask in this context whether there is an implicit distinction between the intrinsic or essential nature (*svabhāva*) of a *dravya* and its *guṇa* (and *paryāya*). This point will be taken up below (p. 23).

The question of the permanent and eternal existence of *dravya* is of fundamental significance to its essential nature, despite its apparent change and 'destruction'. In fact, origination, permanence and destruction of a particular *dravya* can only take place in the context of a particular *dravya* itself, paradoxical as this may sound. In Kundakunda's own words:

> *na bhavo bhaṅga-vihīno bhaṅgo vā na-asti saṃbhava-vihīnaḥ |*
> *utpādo'pi ca bhaṅgo na vinā dhrauvyeṇārtheṇa* || PrS II, 8.
>
> There can be no origination without destruction, nor is there destruction without origination; origination and destruction are not possible in the absence of permanent substantiality.

The key to understanding the occurrence of change on the basis of substantiality is the recognition of the distinction between *paryāya* and *dravya*, which together with *guṇa* are inextricably linked together, as seen above. In other words, the *paryāya* (which functions as a substrate for modifications) of a *dravya*, in no way alters the *dravyatva* of a *dravya* — destruction, permanence and origination have to be seen as *paryāyas* which occur within a *dravya.* This seems to be the import of Kundakunda's statement when he says:

utpāda-sthiti-bhaṅgā vidyante paryāyeṣu paryāyāḥ |
dravyaṃ hi santi niyataṃ tasmād dravyaṃ bhavati sarvam || PrS II, 9.

Origination, permanence and destruction take place in modifications; modifications are (possible) necessarily in a substance, therefore the substance forms the base of them all.

This point raises questions about the relation and interrelation between *dravya* and *paryāya*. In Kundakunda's words:

... svabhāve dravyaṃ dravya-artha-paryāya-arthābhyām |
sad-asad-bhāva-nibaddhaṃ prādur bhāvam sadā labhate || PrS II, 19.

... the substance forever retains its position, in its own nature, as endowed with positive and negative conditions according as it is looked at from the substantial and the modificational view-points.[13]

Two *gāthās*, PrS II, 22–23, elaborate this point which rests on the famous *nayavāda*, the theory of standpoints which has become the hallmark of Jainism:

dravyārthikena sarvaṃ dravyaṃ tat-paryāya-arthikena punaḥ |
bhavati ca-anyad-ananyat tat-kāle tan-mayatvāt ||
astīti ca nāstīti ca bhavaty avaktavyam iti punar dravyam |
paryāyeṇa tu kenāpi tad-ubhayam ādiṣṭam anyad vā || PrS II, 22–23.

All substances are non-different from the substantial view-point, but again they are different from the modificational view-point, because of the individual modification pervading it for the time being. / According to some modification or the other it is stated that a substance exists, does not exist, is indescribable, is both or otherwise.

The distinction between *dravya* and *paryāya* depends on the standpoint from which one approaches the question and although Kundakunda refers only to these two categories one has to keep in mind PrS II, 3 above where it is clearly stated that *guṇa* too is inextricably associated with *dravya*. *Guṇa* is perhaps to be understood as an intermediary category which gives a substance the quality that enables it to become modified without the loss of its substantiality. Thus, the perspective from which one approaches the subject is particularly

[13] 11 The word omitted here is *evaṃ vidham* "in this manner" which continues from the previous *gāthā* (PrS II, 18) which argues that *dravya* is "existence itself" (*dravyaṃ svayaṃ sattā*).

important so as not to make Kundakunda's fine distinction sound absurd or contradictory. In characterising a thing one has to grant that if it can change its form then its substantiality is not in any way diminished, since what it changes into is also described as being a substance, essentially identical with the 'original' substance. When one, on the other hand, considers a substance only from the standpoint of the modifications it undergoes, then there can be total difference between its different states, i.e., before and after the modification. The theory of standpoints, *naya-vāda*, with its corollary *syād-vāda* or *sapta-bhaṅgī*, is a highly developed theory in Jainism through which an absolutistic position is sought to be logically avoided. Kundakunda does not deal with this theory in detail here but he acknowledges its validity only by pointing out that a substance can be said to change or not, depending on the standpoint from which such statements are made.

The notion of *guṇa* is described as a characteristic sign or mark (*liṅga*) of a *dravya*: "The characteristics by which the sentient and non-sentient substances are recognised are known as the special qualities called *mūrta* and *amūrta*, concrete and non-concrete" (*liṅgair yair dravyaṃ jīvo'jīvaś ca bhavati vijñātam | te'tad-bhāva-viśiṣṭā mūrtāmūrtā guṇā jñeyāḥ ||* Prs II, 38). This *gāthā* gives the impression that the *liṅga* of a *dravya* is synonymous with its *guṇa*, even though it is described as a *viśiṣṭa-guṇa*. Unfortunately, Kundakunda does not clearly distinguish these two in the context of *dravya* and the question remains whether, on the other hand, *liṅga* and *paryāya* are identical.[14]

[14] If one considers the example of smoke and fire then, as Nyāya points out, smoke is the *liṅga* of fire and here it is difficult to see how smoke can be seen as the *guna* of fire, which heat and light can be. Further, if smoke were to be the *guṇa* of fire it should always manifest itself whenever fire occurs, which is not so in the case of fire without smoke. The cognition of smoke only indicates the effect of fire, but the presence of fire itself does not necessarily indicate the existence of smoke. This means that fire with smoke

In *gāthās* II, 40–42 the two forms of *guṇa* given above are described. The classification of *guṇa* into *mūrta* and *amūrta* types does not depend on whether the *dravya* is *jīva* or *ajīva* (sentience alone is the criterion for this division) but rather on whether they are empirical, i.e., *pudgala*, or not. The *mūrta-guṇas* are enumerated in II, 40: "Colour taste, smell and touch are found in matter from the finer molecules to the gross earth; and sound is material and of various kinds" (*varṇa-rasa-gandha-sparśā vidyante pudgalasya sūkṣmatvāt* | *pṛthivī-paryantasya ca śabdaḥ sa pudgalaś citraḥ* || PrS II, 40). The *amūrta-guṇa*, as given in the next two *gāthās* are:

ākāśasya avagāho dharma-dravyasya gamana-hetutvam |
dharmetara-dravyasya tu guṇah, punaḥ sthāna-kāraṇatā ||
kālasya vartanā syād guṇa upayoga iti ātmano bhaṇitaḥ |
jñeyāḥ saṃkṣepād guṇā hi mūrti-prahīṇānām || PrS II, 41–42).

"The peculiar property of Ākāśa is to give room; of the Dharma-substance, to be a cause of movement; of Adharma, to be a cause of stationariness; of Kāla, to mark the continuity; of soul, the manifestation of consciousness; these are to be known, in short, the peculiar characteristics of non-concrete substances".[15]

---

would, in Jaina terminology, be one *paryāya* of fire, and fire without smoke the other. Both these types of fire would have at least heat as a *guṇa*. Thus, *liṅga* would be a *paryāya*, fire in its specific mode with smoke. But Kundakunda does not deal with this question here and one is perhaps to assume that *liṅga* is not used in such a technical sense, though a clarification would have made the definition precise.

[15] The Jainas also have a classification of 5 *asti-kāyas*, i.e. of "those entities that manifest, through numerous qualities and modes their existence with extensive spatial points", Upadhye's introduction to *Pravacana-sāra* p. 40. Of the 6 *dravyas* in Jaina metaphysics (5 *ajīva-dravyas* and *jīva-dravya*) only *kāla* is excluded here because there are no space-points in time (*na santi pradeśā iti kālasya*), as PrS II, 43 points out (II, 46 also says the same with reference to a moment, the smallest unit of time, *samayas tv apradeśaḥ*). It is significant to note the plural number of "space- points" because II, 49 says that "time has only one space-point, viz., *samaya*, instant or moment". It is interesting to note how the smallest unit of time (*samaya*) is measured: "it is equal to the time required by that unit of substance measured by one *pradeśa* to traverse one space-point of the sky-substance (... *pradeśa-mātrasya dravya-jātasya* | *vyatipatataḥ sa vartate pradeśam ākāśa-dravyasya* || PrS II, 46).

The concept of *dravya* as represented by Kundakunda is in keeping with the consistent Jaina attempt to avoid an absolutistic stand: a *dravya* is a permanently existing reality insofar as it cannot be destroyed. However, it is not like the Advaitin's eternally existing *brahman* or *ātman* insofar as, in the Jaina view, a *dravya* is also said to undergo change, as seen above. On the other hand, the change that a *dravya* is capable of undergoing is also not absolutised and from this standpoint the Jaina view avoids the Buddhist notion of eternal change embodied in *kṣaṇika-vāda*. Upadhye summarizes the Jaina view of substance succinctly and compares it with the Nyāya view:

> The substances are not immutable but subjected to constant changes in their qualities and modifications with which they are endowed. A substance divested of qualities and modifications is merely an abstraction, simply a void, and as such is not accepted in Jainism. The Nyāya school, however, accepts that the substances, just at the moment of their creation, are devoid of qualities which come to be intimately related with them only later. Substance is the substratum of qualities and modifications; and the intelligibility of a substance depends on its qualities and modifications, because they are its determinants. The relation between these three is that of non-separateness because they subsist in the same spatial extense, and of non-identity because one is not the other.[16]

By virtue of its intrinsic nature a substance (*dravya*) possesses a quality (*guṇa*) which expresses itself in a particular mode (*paryāya*). It is in this sense that the permanent substance can change. The Jainas do not take the further step and talk of a substance per se. This would be unintelligible in an absolute sense. Besides, how can one talk of a substance without at the same time referring to the qualities and modes through which one recognizes it? Further, no outside intervention needs to be acknowledged to account for a substance taking on a particular mode — it can change by virtue of its intrinsic nature to be able to do so.

---

[16] See Upadhye 1984, Introduction to *Pravacana-sāra*, p. 62.

The question of the intrinsic nature of *svabhāva* of a *dravya* takes on a particular significance in the context of *jīva-dravya*, which is the only sentient principle in Jaina ontology. It was asked above whether there is an implicit distinction between the *svabhāva* of a *dravya* and its *guṇa* and *paryāya*. Two *gāthās* need to be quoted here in order to give the context in which Kundakunda uses the term *svabhāva*, before proceeding with the discussion in the context of *jīva-dravya*:

> *jāyate naiva na naśyati kṣaṇa-bhaṅga-samudbhāve jane kaścit* |
> *yo hi bhavaḥ sa vilayaḥ sambhava-vilayāv iti tau nānā* ||
> *tasmāt tu nāsti kaścit svabhāva-samavasthita iti saṃsāre* |
> *saṃsāraḥ punaḥ kriyā samsārato dravyasya* || PrS II, 27–28.
>
> In this world, in which modifications originate and pass away at every moment, nothing is absolutely produced or destroyed; what is production of one modification is the destruction of another; and thus origination and destruction are different. In this world, therefore, there is nothing as such absolutely established in its nature; after all mundane existence is (only) an activity of the soul-substance which is moving (in four grades of existence).

The crucial statement here is that in the world "there is nothing as such which is absolutely established in its nature". In the context of the point under discussion it means that the *jīva* can never be as itself because if it is in the world it is always tainted by *karman*. Kundakunda's description of the *jīva* is:

> *arasam arūpam agandham avyaktaṃ cetana-aguṇam aśabdam* |
> *jānīhy-aliṅga-grahaṇaṃ jīvam anirdiṣṭa-saṃsthānam* || PrS II, 80
>
> Know that the (pure) soul is without (the qualities of) taste, colour, smell, touch and sound; it is sentient; it is beyond inferential mark; and it has no definite shape.

This obviously refers to the *svabhāva* of *jīva* although the *gāthā* does not explicitly state it. The distinction then between the *svabhāva* of a *dravya* and its *guṇa* and *paryāya* seems to be that the *svabhāva* of a *dravya* serves as a definition, i.e., it gives the exact meaning which may be applied to a *dravya*, it says what it is. *Guṇa* and *paryāya*, on the other hand, explain how it is possible to account for the change a *dravya* may undergo without losing its essential nature, its *svabhāva* — without knowing the *svabhāva*, the significance of *guṇa* and *paryāya* to account for the change in a *dravya* would be reduced. Further, *svabhāva* can stand alone whereas *guṇa* and *paryāya* mutually refer to each other with reference to a *dravya*.

The *gāthā* quoted above raises a problem: if, as it says, the *jīva* is without a *liṅga*, then it seems to contradict what was stated in PrS II, 38 above, viz., that the *liṅga* is the special *guṇa* through which *jīva* and *ajīva dravyas* are recognised.

This apparent contradiction can perhaps be obviated by clarifying the standpoint from which these statements are made: recognition is a faculty that takes place in the world, i.e., it is a manifestation of sentience albeit under the influence of matter, since *jīva* is under the influence of *pudgala-dravya* transformed as *karman* which has the effect of restricting the manifestation of the intrinsic nature of the *jīva*. It is in this sense that the *jīva* can be understood as not being established in its nature. The intrinsic nature of the *jīva* can only be grasped when the *karman* veiling its authentic manifestation has been cleared. However, even under the influence of *karman* sentience, *jīvatva*, is manifested and the operation of consciousness in the form, e.g., of recognition, is a sign of its existence. Hence, on the one hand, the *jīva* is recognized in the world through its characteristic signs of sentience and, on the other hand, in the realm without the influence of *karman*, i.e., in the realm where the *ajīva-dravyas* no longer hinder the manifestation of consciousness, *jīva* must be spoken of as a *dravya* which cannot be recognized through characteristic signs or *liṅgas* which apply to the realm associated with *ajīva*.

The Jaina scriptures enumerate two operations (*upayogas*) which are described as two distinct *guṇas* of the *jīva*, and these are called *darśana* and *jñāna*. A full discussion of *upayogas* in Jainism and the different views concerning them is the subject matter of the detailed study in the next chapter. Only some important points will be touched upon for the context here here. *Darśana* is described as indeterminate intuition (*nirākāra-upayoga*) and *jñāna* as determinate knowledge (*sākāra-upayoga*). "The two operate always in succession (*krama*), with *darśana* first, for all acts of cognition in the mundane state".[17] The question which has transformed this point into a problem is whether *darśana* and *jñāna* maintain their distinctness in the state of omniscience. In other words, how is the unity of *jīva-dravya* to be understood when the *jīva* has attained its perfected and natural state? It is interesting to briefly compare Kundakunda's view with that of Siddhasena Divākara whose standpoint on the problem is evidently quite different.

Kundakunda, as seen above, accepts the *bheda-vāda* view, viz., that the *guṇa* and *paryāya* of a *dravya* are distinct entities. Further, *guṇa* is embedded in a *dravya* and it is called *saha-bhāvi*, intrinsic to and acknowledged simultaneously with a *dravya*. A *paryāya* is a feature manifesting itself in a *dravya* for a time and changing into another *paryāya* at some other time. In this sense *paryāya* is a relatively extrinsic feature and is called *krama-bhāvi* or successive. *Jñāna* and *darśana* are *guṇas* of the *jīva* and in the perfected state of omniscience these must also function as separate operations without the *jīva* losing its identity. But if, as stated above, *darśana* and *jñāna* operate successively, then it would mean that the omniscient one (by which is meant the Jina) would always be deprived of one or the other of these qualities, even though both qualities are in a perfected, unhindered condition. Kundakunda's solution to the problem is that although these operations function successively in the mundane or *vyavahārika* state, in the state of omniscience they operate simultaneously (*yugapat*). Kundakunda's *bheda-vāda* is generally supported by Umāsvāti, Pūjyapāda and Vidyānandin and represents the Digambara view on the matter.

[17] P. S. Jaini's introduction to Amṛtacandrasūri's *Laghutattvasphoṭa*, p. 18.

Siddhasena Divākara (*c.* 500 CE), on the other hand, in his *Sanmati-tarka-prakaraṇa* (III, 8–14), maintains the *abheda-vāda* view, viz., that the *guṇa* and *paryāya* of a *dravya* are not different because they are synonyms (*tulyārtha*). Either of these terms may be employed when referring to the change a *dravya* undergoes and in III, 10 he relies on *śruti* for his standpoint. He says that scripture refers only to *dravyārthika-naya* and *paryāyārthika-naya* and that Lord Mahāvīra does not mention *guṇārthika-naya* as a separate feature associated with a *dravya*. This means that *guṇa* has to be understood in the sense of *paryāya*. Further, there is no need to consider *guṇa* as a separate aspect that has an independent status because when one speaks of a *dravya* the qualities or *guṇas* are automatically included. In the state of omniscience, then, *darśana* and *jñāna* are not separate operations, they are no longer the distinct features they were in the mundane realm. In other words, they are qualities intrinsic to *jīva* and when it achieves omniscience the *jīva* abides in itself in a perfected state.

Upadhye[18] thinks that Siddhasena Divākara's standpoint is apparently directed against the Nyāya-Vaiśeṣika and includes Jaina authors like Kundakunda and Umāsvāti only in the context of *dravya* and *paryāya*. He thinks that Siddhasena has confused the Nyāya-Vaiśeṣika and Kundakunda positions. He evidently supports Kundakunda and so tries to explain away Siddhasena's objections. His arguments distinguishing Kundakunda's position with regard to *guṇa* from that of Nyāya-Vaiśeṣika, may be mentioned here in order better to understand the Jaina view. According to Kundakunda a *guṇa* is an essential differentia of a substance (*dravya*) and a substance without a *guṇa* has no existence; the relation between *guṇa*

[18] See Upadhye 1984 in his introduction to Kundakunda's *Pravacana-sāra*, p. 64. The summary that follows is largely based on the section he entitles 'Kundakunda's position stated and Siddhasena's objections explained away', *ibid*.

and *dravya* is that of difference-in-congruency. According to the Nyāya school, however, a substance in the first moment of its creation is without qualities, and only in the next moment does it come to be intimately united with them. Secondly, many of the Nyāya-Vaiśeṣika *guṇas* like *śabda*, etc. are no more *guṇas* according to Jainism, but merely forms of matter. Lastly, the qualitative difference in atoms corresponding to earth, water, fire, and air as accepted by Vaiśeṣika is not possible according to Jainism.

After distinguishing the two views Upadhye goes on to clarify Kundakunda's position and to consider Siddhasena's view. He first illustrates Kundakunda's distinction between *guṇa* and *paryāya*: if one considers a golden pot and an earthen pot, then the *paryāya*, pot, is the same but the *guṇas* or qualities of gold and earth are not the same. Moreover, if one considers a golden ring and a golden bangle then the qualities with the substratum gold are the same but the *paryāyas* are different. Siddhasena's argument against this is that if the *guṇa* and *paryāya* of a *dravya* are indeed different then why do the scriptures not mention *guṇārthika-naya*? By way of answering this objection Upadhye gives a lucid summary of the problem at hand.

He says: the *paryāya* is an external imposition, it may be of manifold kinds, the same *paryāya* may be possible on different substance-grounds, the same substance may be subjected to different *paryāyas* at different times; and, the *paryāya* is not essentially inherent in the very nature of the substance (in the sense in which a *guṇa* is). The only relation between a *dravya* and a *paryāya* is that a *dravya* cannot be imagined without one or the other *paryāya*. *Paryāya* stands for the fluctuating aspect of substances and qualities and requires to be stated when anything is to be said about a substance, hence, the necessity of *paryāyārthika-naya*. As distinguished from this, the *dravyārthika-naya* is directed not towards the fluctuating aspect of a thing but to the permanent aspect of it, namely to the substance with qualities. A *guṇa* cannot be perceived anywhere else than in a substance, and a substance cannot be conceived without a *guṇa*. Since the *guṇas* are embedded in and coeval with a substance there is no need for a *guṇārthika-naya*. This would be necessary, Upadhye points out, if the Jainas like the Naiyāyikas admitted the possibility of substance without *guṇas*, at least for a while.

In conclusion Upadhye makes a textual reference in order finally to explain away Siddhasena's objection. Colour, taste, smell and touch are the qualities of matter or *pudgala* and being inherent and essential characteristics of matter they continue to remain even up to the stage of primary atoms. But qualities too have their *paryāyas* or modes: colour as a quality has the five modifications black, blue, yellow, white and red.[19] So the phrase *vaṇṇapajjavehim* (*Bhagavatīsūtra* 4, 513) means "by the modifications of colour" and there is no implication here at all that the colour is a *paryāya*. If the word were to be taken as a Karmadhāraya compound then the plural loses its force, *vaṇṇa* as a quality being only one. The conclusion he thus comes to is that it is justified to draw the distinction between *guṇa* and *paryāya*. And then he adds: moreover we do find passages in the Śvetāmbara canon itself where the *guṇa* and *paryāya* of a *dravya* are distinguished, namely in *Uttarādhyayana-sūtra* 28, 6.

In Jainism the discussion on *dravya*, *guṇa* and *paryāya* has been an ongoing one and what has been touched upon here are the basic points of the problem with special reference to Kundakunda. Not only do the details discussed above evince

---

[19] In a footnote on this point Upadhye acknowledges the confusion in sometimes referring to a colour as both *guṇa* and *paryāya*. The original Jaina idea, he adds, was that colour is a *guṇa* and the different colours such as yellow, etc., are *paryāyas* of that *guṇa*. The confusion arose because according to Vaiśeṣika the various colours are *guṇas*.

the Jaina intensive concern with the philosophical implications of the subject, but they also show how consistent the Jainas were in applying the concepts of substance, etc. to both the sentient and insentient substances. The crux of the problem is that changes are accounted for in both, without the substances losing their intrinsic substance-ness in any way, as repeatedly said.

Their epistemological significance lies in the fact that the insentient categories are the objects that are to be cognised (*prameya*), like pots, etc. and what cognises (*pramātr*) is the sentient category *jīva*. In the process of cognition, what cognises 'undergoes' changes in it without relinquishing its sentience. This is unique to Jainism and can be compared, *mutatis mutandis*, with the role of *cic-chakti* in Śaivism, particularly in Śaiva Siddhānta.[20] This means that, in fact, the proper means of cognition (*pramāṇa*) in Jainism is the *jīva* itself. This is the function, operation or faculty (*upayoga*) of the *jīva*, during which it does not at all relinquish its *jīvatva*. This is what the next chapter explicates in more detail.

[20] See Soni 1989, especially pp. 100–119.

Chapter 3
Upayoga
Its unique function for cognition and knowledge

In the previous chapter the epistemological significance of *upayoga* was established on the basis of the terms substance (*dravya*), quality (*guṇa*) and the mode or modification (*paryāya*) which a substance undergoes or takes on. The last of these was linked to *upayoga*. The term *upayoga* applies only to the sentient principle *jīva*. Such an *upayoga* function, application or faculty of sentience does not occur in the *ajīva*-substances, which undergo a mere change or modification of its form, like gold modified into a bangle or ring. However, the link between *paryāya* and *upayoga* enables an understanding of the change that occurs in the sentient principle, without abandoning its sentience.[1]

All standard works on Jaina philosophy have to deal with *upayoga* because it is described as a 'sign' (*lakṣaṇa*) of *jīva* or the sentient principle.[2] As such a 'sign' of the sentient principle, the concept of *upayoga* not only comes within the gamut of ontology but also epistemology, because the terms *jñāna* and *darśana* are said to be *upayogas*, 'functions, applications or faculties' of the sentient principle. In other words, in manifes-

---

[1] This chapter is based on my "*Upayoga*, according to Kundakunda and Umāsvāti" published in the *Journal of Indian Philosophy*, 2007, 35: 299–311. I thank the Springer "Copyright Clearance Center" for kindly allowing me to reuse the article, email dated 6 October 2016.

[2] The translation 'soul' which is often used for *jīva* is avoided here, apart from quotations. The original word *jīva* or 'sentient principle' is preferred.

ting itself *upayoga* would be identical with the functions of *darśana* and/or *jñāna*. Precisely herein lies the problem: what are these functions exactly and do they take place simultaneously? If they take place in sequence, which function takes place first and what is its status in relation to the other? Does each have a separate identity, i.e., can each operate without the function of the other? Further, what is the precise difference between say *jñāna* as an *upayoga* and *jñāna* as a *pramāṇa*?

This chapter attempts to deal with the concept of *upayoga* as it is described in selected works, including what can be found in the canon, and then to highlight the controversies which subsequently arose. An attempt will also be made to draw a clear distinction between *upayoga* as a *lakṣaṇa* or 'sign' of the sentient principle (i.e., *upayoga* in the context of ontology) and *upayoga* as a part of the *pramāṇas* (i.e., *upayoga* in the context of epistemology, where usually only *jñāna* alone is mentioned, not *darśana*).[3] For the purposes here special attention will be paid to comparing the views of Umāsvāti, Kundakunda and, briefly, Vidyānandin on this issue.

The text one usually consults at the outset for matters dealing with Jaina philosophy is Umāsvāti's *Tattvārtha-sūtra* (TS). This is the first Sanskrit work (certainly before the fourth -fifth centuries CE) which deals with Jaina philosophy in a manner comparable to the basic *sūtra* works of the other schools of Indian philosophy.[4] Furthermore, Umāsvāti is the

---

[3] *Tattvārtha-sūtra* 1, 9 says that *mati, śruta, avadhi, manaḥ-paryāya* and *kevala* (these five) are *jñāna* and TS 1, 10 that these constitute the two *pramāṇas* (*tat-pramāṇe*), the first two of the list are *parokṣa* (TS 1, 11 *ādye parokṣam*) and the rest *pratyakṣa* (*pratyakṣam anyat*, TS 1, 12). Note that *darśana* does not feature here. However, afterwards, in the commentaries to TS 2, 9, we learn that *maty-ajñāna, śrutājñāna*, and *vibhaṅga-jñāna* (= *avadhy-ajñāna*) should also be taken into account. It is to be noted that in the commentaries to TS 2, 9 *darśana* is mentioned in addition to *jñāna*, see below. TS 1, 31/32 which says the same, without reference to *upayoga*.

[4] See Ohira 1982 for details about the problems related especially to the

authority for both Digambaras and Śvetāmbaras, enjoying a revered status in the Jaina tradition similar to Śaṅkara's for Vedānta. The next step when dealing with a particular problem would be to see what the canonical texts say on the issue and then to broaden the investigation by comparing these with other views in the tradition, e.g., with those of Kundakunda and Vidyānandin. This is what will be attempted here.

Chapter 2 of Umāsvāti's work mainly deals with the category of *jīva,* and TS 2, 8 here says merely *upayogo lakṣaṇam*, which means that *upayoga* is the 'sign' (of the sentient principle), translated by Jain 1992: 55 as: "Consciousness is the differentia (distinctive characteristic) of the soul." Here *upayoga* is rendered as "consciousness", which is also the usual translation of *cit* or *caitanya*. The question of an adequate translation of this and other terms will be a major problem and in the course of this investigation help will be sought from relevant sections of commentaries to try and find out what the technical terms entail.[5] In his commentary to this TS 2, 8 just quoted, Pūjyapāda says in his *Sarvārtha-siddhi* (SS):

> *ubhaya-nimittavaśād utpadyamānaś caitanyānuvidhāyī pariṇāma upayogaḥ* | *tena bandhaṃ pratyekatve saty apy ātmā lakṣyate suvarṇa-rajatayor bandhaṃ pratyekatve saty api varṇādi-bhedavat* |

---

commentary and its authorship — the Digambaras (who also refer to the author as Umāsvāmin) say that Pūjyapāda wrote the first commentary and the Śvetāmbaras (who refer to the text also as *Tattvārthādhigama-sūtra*) say that Umāsvāti wrote an auto-commentary called *Svopajña-bhāṣya*. See also Soni 2003a for further aspects related to this basic Jaina philosophical work and ibid. p. 32 for the reference to the Digambara and Śvetāmbara versions of the TS. Unless otherwise stated all references to Umāsvāti's *Tattvārtha-sūtra* and the translation of Pūjyapāda's commentary on it called *Sarvārtha-siddhi* (SS) are quoted from Jain 1992. The corresponding Sanskrit texts of Pūjyapāda's *SS* are quoted from the 1955 ed.

[5] Deleu 1996: 94 translates *uvaoga/upayoga* as "spiritual function"; Tatia 1951: 70 as "consciousness"; Shah 1971: 399 and Jaini 1979: 104 as "cognition". The dictionary meanings of *upayoga* include such translations as "employment, use, application". The meaning "acquisition (of knowledge)" would also apply in the context dealt with here.

> That [transformation], which arises from both internal and external causes and concomitant with consciousness, is *upayoga* (active or attentive consciousness). By this the soul is distinguished from the body, though it is one with the body from the point of view of bondage, just as gold and silver are distinct by their colour, etc. though mixed together (tr. Jain 1992: 55).

This commentary says explicitly that consciousness (*caitanya*) undergoes two forms of transformations, that these transformations maintain the essential nature of consciousness as such, and that these transformations, which are a sign of two kinds of activity within consciousness itself, serve implicitly as a specific feature distinguishing consciousness from non-consciousness. This is obviously the basic point of Jaina ontology where the *jīva* is distinguished from *ajīva*. In other words, what we have here in the context of *upayoga* is a further specification of the intrinsic nature of the sentient principle, which can be seen as a combination of two of its three main qualities (*guṇa*), namely, *caitanya* (consciousness), and *vīrya* (energy, the third being *sukha*):[6] because the sentient principle possesses energy as one of its natures consciousness (which is also intrinsic to the sentient principle) is in a position to transform itself on account of this energy. Consciousness can do this without losing its intrinsic nature. This means that the consciousness inherent to the *jīva* has the ability to transform itself, that the transformation is termed *upayoga*, and that this *upayoga*, as we shall presently see, manifests itself as *jñāna* and *darśana*.

---

[6] For a brief summary of the intrinsic nature of the sentient principle see Jaini 1979: 104–106. Technically speaking *upayoga* is a *lakṣaṇa* of *jīva* and not its *guṇa* (like *caitanya* is, for example). However, *upayoga* can be seen as a *lakṣaṇa* of *caitanya*. In this case the function or application (*upayoga*) would be the sign (*lakṣaṇa*) of consciousness which is a quality (*guṇa*) of the sentient principle. The former presupposes the latter, because without consciousness there cannot be its function. In other words, by definition *guṇa* and *lakṣaṇa* can be used synonymously in some contexts, in the sense of 'quality, peculiarity, attribute or property' and 'mark, sign, symbol and characteristic attribute' respectively.

TS 2, 9 and its commentary are more specific as regards the different kinds of *upayoga*: *sa dvividho 'ṣṭa-catur-bhedaḥ*, "Consciousness [*upayoga*] is of two kinds. And these in turn are of eight and four kinds respectively." Pūjyapāda's commentary in the translation by Jain 1992: 55–56 elaborates the point made here:

> "Consciousness [*upayoga*] is of two kinds, knowledge [*jñānopayoga*] and perception [*darśanopayoga*]. Knowledge is of eight kinds, sensory knowledge [*mati*], scriptural knowledge [*śruta*], clairvoyance [*avadhi*], telepathy [*manaḥ-paryāya*], omniscience [*kevala*], wrong sensory knowledge [*maty-ajñāna*], wrong scriptural knowledge [*śrutājñāna*] and wrong clairvoyance [*vibhaṅga-jñāna*]. Perception is of four kinds, perception through the eyes [*cakṣur-darśana*], perception by the senses other than the eyes [*acakṣur-dar°*], clairvoyant perception [*avadhi-dar°*] and omniscient perception [*kevala-dar°*]. How are these, knowledge [*jñānopayoga*] and perception [*darśanopayoga*], different? The one (knowledge) is with details [*sākāra*], and the other (perception) without details [*anākāra*]. Apprehension of the mere object (the universal) is perception, and awareness of the particulars is knowledge. These occur in succession in ordinary mortals (non-omniscients), but simultaneously in those who have annihilated karmas. Though perception occurs first, knowledge being more worthy is mentioned first. ..."[7]

[7] The Sanskrit text is: *sa upayogo dvi-vidhaḥ: — jñanopayogo darśanopayogaś ceti | jñanopayogo 'ṣṭabhedaḥ — mati-jñānaṃ śruta-jñānam avadhi-jñānaṃ manaḥ-paryāya-jñānaṃ kevala-jñānaṃ maty-ajñānaṃ śrutājñānaṃ vibhaṅga-jñānaṃ ceti | darśanopayogaś catur-vidhaḥ — cakṣur-darśanam acakṣur-darśanam avadhi-darśanaṃ kevala-darśanaṃ ceti | tayoḥ kathaṃ bhedaḥ? sākārānākāra-bhedāt | sākāraṃ jñānam anākaraṃ darśanam iti | tac chad-mastheṣu krameṇa vartate | nirāvaraṇeṣu yugapat pūrva-kāla-bhāvino 'pi darśanāj jñānasya prāgupanyāsaḥ; abhyarhitatvāt* | ... Umāsvāti's *Svopajña-bhāṣya* begins the commentary to this *sūtra* 2, 9 in this way (p. 82 of the 1932 ed.): *sa upayogo dvi-vidhaḥ sākāro 'nākāraś ca jñanopayogo darśanopayogaś cety arthaḥ*: 'The meaning (of the *sūtra*) is: *upayoga* is of two kinds, *sākāra* and *anākāra* which [respectively] are *jñānopayoga* and *darśanopayoga*.' The commentary then continues with the division of these into eight and four types. The *Svopajña-bhāṣya* (unlike the SS) does not say anything about the occurrence of *upayoga*. An inquiry into the details about the differences here between Pūjyapāda's and Umāsvāti's commentaries will have to be postponed — see here again Ohira 1982.

For the context of the point here TS 2, 9 has to be compared with TS 1, 9–13 which state that the five terms *mati, śruta, avadhi, manaḥ-paryāya* and *kevala* all together constitute *jñāna*, and that *jñāna* as a whole in the context of the *sūtras* 1, 9-10 is in fact equivalent to the two types of means or instruments of cognition (*pramāṇa*; *darśana* does not feature at all here in the context of *pramāṇa*). The first two of the list of five are called *parokṣa-jñāna* (indirect means of cognition, TS 1, 11) and the remaining three are called *pratyakṣa-jñāna* (direct means of cognition, TS 1, 12).[8]

In trying to understand TS 1, 9–13 and TS 2, 9 the following conclusions seem evident: all five terms of TS 1, 9 plus the first three terms in their negative forms, constitute the eight types of *upayogas* of *jñāna* in TS 2, 9. Further, *avadhi* and *kevala* can also manifest themselves as *upayogas* of *darśana* and together with visual and non-visual perceptions *darśanopayoga* is said to be of four types. Whilst TS 2, 9 takes over all the terms mentioned in TS 1, 9 and adding a few others, the word *jñāna* used in TS 1, 9 is expressly in the sense of a means or instrument of knowledge or *pramāṇa* (in which *darśana*, as just pointed out, does not feature at all in the context of *pramāṇa*). TS 2, 9, on the other hand, uses the term *jñāna* as one of the two *upayogas* of *jīva*, and not in the purely epistemological context of TS 1, 9.[9] It is noteworthy that in TS 2, 8 Umāsvāti uses only the word

---

[8] TS 1, 13 supplies four synonyms for the term *mati*, like memory and recognition, which do not concern us here at the moment.

[9] Pūjyapāda hints at the reference to TS 1, 9 in his commentary to TS 2, 9 when he says: *samyag-jñāna-prakaraṇāt pūrvaṃ pañca-vidho jñanopayogo vyākhyātaḥ | iha punar upayoga-grahaṇād viparyayo 'pi gṛhyate ity aṣṭa-vidha iti ucyate |* 'Since there was a section dealing with right knowledge (*samyag-jñāna*) [TS 1] the *upayoga* of *jñāna* was dealt with as being fivefold [as in TS 1, 9]. Here, in taking up *upayoga* again misapprehension/error is also being handled, [with *jñānopayoga*] being said to be eightfold.' Jain 1992:56 translates: "In the section dealing with right knowledge, the five kinds of right knowledge were explained formerly. But here, the wrong kinds of knowledge are also mentioned, as this is the section dealing with consciousness in general. Hence it is mentioned as of eight kinds."

upayoga alone, without the terms *jñāna* and *darśana* as *upayogas* — only the commentaries spell them out (see p. 35 above).

In the light of what has been said so far with regard to the topic in the TS the following distinctions have to be made with regard to *darśana* and *jñāna* in the work as a whole:

1. TS 1, 1 says *samyag-darśana-jñāna-cāritrāṇi mokṣa-mārgaḥ*, where *darśana* and *jñāna* are two of three constituents which together make up the path to liberation; *darśana* and *jñāna* apparently have an indirect and limited reference to their functions or operations as *upayogas*. Here *darśana* and *jñāna* would not include the negative aspects of their functions mentioned in the commentary to TS 2, 9, because the path to *mokṣa* essentially can only be positive. Further, the use of the word *jñāna* in TS 1, 1 is not used in the epistemological context of TS 1, 9.
2. The word *jñāna* in TS 1, 9 is used in the general sense of *pramāṇa*, where five means of knowledge are enumerated as comprising the two groups of *pratyakṣa* and *parokṣa* (the term *darśana* playing no role at all in this context). That the term *jñāna* here in TS 1, 9 can also be seen as an *upayoga* is hinted at only later, in the commentary to TS 2, 9, with the proviso that now in TS 2, 9 it is necessary to also include the negative aspects of *jñāna* not mentioned in TS 1, 9, and that in TS 2, 9 *darśana* is mentioned together with *jñāna* as an *upayoga*.
3. TS 2, 9 wants to accommodate the condition for the possibility of error as an intrinsic function of *jñāna* so as to account for probable cases of incorrect apprehension of the basic Jaina tenets — the truth or falsity of a doctrine can be finally established on the basis of what is laid down in the canon. In both true and false cases the function of knowledge can only be on the part of the self-same *jīva*. The commentary to TS 2, 9 explicitly makes room for error when *jñānopayoga* takes place, i.e, when the function of *jñā-*

na manifests itself (keeping in mind that in TS 1, 9 *darśana* is not mentioned). Such an interpretation would explain the condition for the possibility of having false insights despite the fact that one follows the Jaina principles. This is expressly mentioned in the special context of *upayoga* where both *darśana* and *jñāna* are involved, including the possibility of false insights.

4. One further significant point is derived from Pūjyapāda's commentary to TS 2, 9: after establishing that *upayoga* is a faculty of *jīva* and that it manifests itself as *jñāna* and *darśana*, it is said that *jñāna* is knowledge (in the sense of cognition) which is 'with a form or is specific' (*sākāra*) and that *darśana* is cognition which is 'without a form or is unspecific' (*anākāra*), both kinds of knowledge taking place in the sentient principle. Umāsvāti's *Svopajña-bhāṣya* begins with this distinction at the very outset (see fn. 7). In other words, the introduction of the terms *sākāra* and *anākāra* blurs the strict distinction between *upayoga* as a sign of the sentient principle (in the sense of an intrinsic function or ability associated with *caitanya*), and the role of the instruments of knowledge or *pramāṇa* (see under Vidyānandin below for more on this point). The introduction here of the terms *sākāra* and *anākāra* require some explanation which would now take us back to the Jaina canon.

In the Jaina tradition any discussion of the sentient principle, including the occurrence of *jñāna* and *darśana* in it, is inextricable from the notion of concealing karmas (*āvaraṇīya-karma*). This idea goes back to the beginnings of Jaina thought and can be traced also in the earliest canonical works of the tradition. For our purposes here it is necessary to note that in the case of the faculty of *upayoga* its manifestation as *jñāna* and *darśana* is always obscured in the case of unliberated beings. In other words, it would be interesting to see what the Jaina canon says about the issue at hand. The terms *sākāra* and *anākāra* mentioned above appear there, and the main distinction is not between *darśana* and *jñāna* but rather between *upayoga* and *paśyattā*.

What directly concerns us here are chapters 29 (*uvaoga-payaṃ/upayoga-padam*) and 30 (*pāsaṇayā-payaṃ/paśyattā-padam*) of the *Paṇṇavaṇā-suttaṃ/Prajñāpanā-sūtram*, the fourth *Upāṅga* of the Jaina canon (PraSū), which deal with the categories of *jīva* and *ajīva*:

> *sāgārovaoge ya aṇāgārovaoge ya* (PraSū 29, *sū*. 1908): *Upayoga* is *sākāra* or *anākāra*.
>
> *sāgārapāsaṇayā aṇāgārapāsaṇayā ya* (PraSū 30, *sū*. 1936): *Paśyattā* is *sākāra* or *anākārà*.[10]

These *sūtras* state explicitly that both *upayoga* and *paśyattā* can be *sākāra* as well as *anākāra*.[11] What is baffling is that at the end of the section dealing with *paśyattā* the text says: *sāgāre se ṇāṇe*

[10] In the 2000 ed. of the PraSū these are *sūtras* 572 and 573 respectively. In introducing these *sūtras* the commentator Malayagiri says (the *sandhis* are supplied as in the printed ed.): (to 29) ... *jñāna-pariṇāma-viśeṣaḥ upayogaḥ pratipadyate...* it (the *sūtra*) regards *upayoga* as a special transformation of *jñāna* and (to 30) ... *jñāna-pariṇāma-viśeṣe upayoge paśyattā cintyate* ... when *upayoga* is a special transformation of knowledge it is thought to be *paśyattā*. In other words like Abhayadeva, Malayagiri considers *paśyattā* to be a special form of *upayoga* (Shah 1971:400 and 401). The word *pāsaṇayā/paśyattā* also appears in the *Viyāha-pannatti (Bhagavaī)*, the fifth Aṅga of the Jaina canon, (also called *Bhagavatī-Aṅga-sūtram* or *Vyākhyā-prajñapti Aṅga-sūtram*) and refers to the PraSū quoted here, see Deleu 1996: 228. Further, the commentator Malayagiri repeats the gist of Abhayadeva's classification of each of the means of cognition that fall under *paśyattā* and *upayoga*. For *sāgārovautta/sākāṛopayoga* Deleu 1996: 122 has "possessing the faculty of concrete imagination" and for *aṇāgāra/anākāra* "abstract imagination"; on p. 147 he says: "distinct and indistinct imagination (*sāgārovautta, aṇāgārovautta*)", and "concrete or abstract imagination" on p. 160 for the same terms; *pāsaṇayā/ paśyattā* is translated as "seeing" on p. 228. Tatia 1951: 70 translates *sākāra* and *anākāra* as "determinate" and "indeterminate" respectively.

[11] Shah 1971: 400 supplies a table comparing the divisions of *upayoga* and *paśyattā* in the PraSū because, as he says, "the text proper does not give the definition of either of them". He mentions the 8 kinds of *sākāropayoga* and 4 kinds of *anākāropayoga* as against six kinds of *sākāra-paśyattā* and three kinds of *anākāra-paśyattā* mentioned in the text.

bhavati aṇāgāre se daṃsaṇe bhavati, seteṇaṭṭheṇaṃ jāva ṇo taṃ samayaṃ jāṇati, the meaning of which is that since *jñāna* is *sākāra* and *darśana* is *anākāra* no one can have *jñāna* and *darśana* simultaneously (PraSū 30, *sū.* 1963, with *sū.* 1964 repeating the same sense). Although this is a reference to a *kevalin*, the point is: why is the term *paśyattā* not used here? It seems that in the absence of anything further on *paśyattā* in the Jaina canon, or elsewhere, the problem can only be raised at the moment with the tentative solution that in post-canonical thought the *upayoga* of the canon becomes *jñāna* and its *paśyattā* becomes *darśana* and that both *jñāna* and *darśana* are designated *upayoga*. The hint for this assumption may be seen from the fact that in the commentary to Umāsvāti (as seen above) only *jñāna* and *darśana* are the *upayogas*. The only source for the distinction between *upayoga* and *paśyattā* is the PraSū quoted above with Malayagiri's commentary.[12]

---

[12] Together with the reference to Abhayadeva, Shah 1971: 401 says that "There are no other sources to know the distinction between *upayoga* and *paśyattā*", i.e., in the Śvetāmbara canon. Tatia 1951: 72 refers to the second-century work *Ṣaṭ-kaṇḍāgama*, the oldest Digambara sacred text, in the same place where he deals with *upayoga* (the title of the section though is *jñāna* and *darśana*). In *sūtra* 1, 1, 4 of the *Ṣaṭkaṇḍāgama* (p. 133, vol. 1) *jñāna* and *darśana* are two of fourteen topics of discussion or inquiry and Vīrasena (eight-ninth century CE) comments on these two terms on pp. 146–150 (the 14 topics are: *gati, indriya, kāya, yoga, veda, kaṣāya, jñāna, samyama, darśana, leśyā, bhavyatva, samyaktva, saṃjñī* and *āhāra*). The word *upayoga* is neither used in the *sūtra* nor in the commentary (only the free translation in Hindī uses it, p. 143), but judging from the content concerning *jñāna* and *darśana* here, the terms seem to be used in the sense of *pramāṇa* or instruments of knowing through which general and specific aspects are cognised: *sāmānya-viśeṣātmaka-bāhyārtha-grahaṇaṃ jñānaṃ, tathātmaka-svarūpa-grahaṇaṃ darśanam iti siddham* |, '*jñāna* is what grasps an external object in its universal and particular natures, *darśana* is what grasps its intrinsic nature' (p. 148).

The commentary here is occupied more with establishing the difference between these terms because the opponent would like to see them as synonyms in the context of cognition. On p. 147 the opponent says: *tato na jñāna-darśanayor bhedaḥ*, 'therefore, there is no difference between *darśana* and *jñāna*,' to which Vīrasena says: *iti cen na, jñānād iva darśanāt prati-karma-vya-*

The next step in terms of what is attempted here is to see what Kundakunda and Vidyānandin have to say on the theme.

In his 1984 edition of Kundakunda's *Pravacanaśāra (Pavayaṇa-sāra)*, Upadhye supplies a useful and exhaustive introduction in English (pp. 1–126) and in it he briefly deals with the "Doctrine of Three Upayogas" (pp. 68–70). He mentions the following *gāthās* related to the topic: I 7, 9, 11–14, 69–70 and 78; II 63–65, 68 and 89; and III 45. Not all of them are directly concerned with the theme in our context here, but the references are useful to have. Upadhye translates *upayoga* as "manifestation of consciousness".

We saw at the beginning and in fn. 10 above that *upayoga* is also regarded as *pariṇāma*, together with the reference to *jñāna* and *darśana* as two such *upayogas* (Kundakunda also uses *upayukta/uvajutta*, for example in PrS III 45). Not only does Kundakunda use all these terms but also *śubha, aśubha* and *śuddha* (auspicious, inauspicious and pure, in I 9 and II 64) with reference to the *pariṇāma* or transformation of the sentient principle. This means that we have an interesting deviation from and addition to the use of *upayoga* so far.

In his *Pravacanasāra* (PraSā) II 63–64 Kundakunda uses the term *upayoga/uvaoga* in this way:[13]

---

vasthābhāvāt, 'if this is said then no, because, in the case of *darśana* there is no distinction with regard to the acts [of cognition], as in the case of *jñāna*', meaning thereby that unlike *darśana, jñāna* grasps the specific aspects of an object. In view of the fact that the word *upayoga* is not used here, the reference to it by Tatia 1951: 72 is interesting from the general point of view of epistemology. (The *Ṣaṭkaṇḍāgama* is based on the oral teaching of a monk called Dharasena and has been published with Vīrasena's renowned ninth-century commentary *Dhavalā*. Dharasena's two disciples, Puṣpadanta and Bhūtabali, committed this 'Scripture in Six Parts' to writing. See Dundas 2002: 65–66 for the remarkable story about the text from a Jaina monastery and the fait accompli of the publication of its early portions. See also Jaini 1979: 50f. on the Digambara canon.)

[13] Unless otherwise stated, the translations below are by Upadhye in his ed. of the work, as given at the end of the edition (pp. 384–410). The ed. conveniently supplies Amṛtacandra's Sanskrit translation of *gāthās* which are also included here.

appā uvaogappā uvaogo ṇāṇadaṃsaṇaṃ bhaṇido |
so vi suho asuho vā uvaogo appaṇo havadi || II 63 ||
ātmā upayogātmā upayogo jñānadarśanaṃ bhaṇitaḥ |
so 'pi śubho 'śubho vā upayoga ātmano bhavati || II 63 ||

"The soul is constituted of the manifestation of consciousness; manifestation of consciousness is towards knowledge and cognition; the manifestation of consciousness of the soul is either auspicious or inauspicious" [tr. p. 399].

uvaogo jadi hi suho puṇṇaṃ jīvassa saṃcayaṃ jādi |
asuho vā tadha pāvaṃ tesim abhāve ṇa cayam atthi || II 64 ||
upayogo yadi hi śubhaḥ puṇyaṃ jīvasya sañcayaṃ yāti |
aśubho vā tathā pāpaṃ tayor abhāve na cayo 'sti || II 64 ||

"If the manifestation of consciousness is auspicious, the soul accumulates merit; if inauspicious, sin; in the absence of both there is no accumulation (of Karmas)" [tr. p. 399].

Since the word *upayoga/uvaoga* is explicitly used here with the reference to "auspicious", etc., the latter terms express the idea of *pariṇāma* or transformation of the soul. That *upayoga* then can be seen as synonymous with *pariṇāma* is evident in PraSā I, 9 where Kundakunda expresses the same idea:

jīvo pariṇamadi jadā suhe a asuheṇa vā suho asuho |
suddheṇa tadā suddho havadi hi pariṇāma-sabbhāvo || I 9 ||
jīvaḥ pariṇamati yadā śubhenāśubhena vā śubho 'śubhaḥ |
śuddhena tadā śuddho bhavati hi pariṇāma-svabhāvaḥ || I 9 ||

"The Soul whose nature is amenable to modification comes to be auspicious, inauspicious or pure according as it develops auspicious, inauspicious or pure states (of consciousness)" [tr. p. 385].

A similar thought is expressed where the word *upayukta/uvajutta* is used:

dhammeṇa pariṇadappā appā jadi suddhasaṃpayogajudo |
pāvadi ṇivvāṇasuhaṃ suhovajutto va saggasuhaṃ || I 11 ||
dharmeṇa pariṇatātmā ātmā yadi śuddhasaṃprayogayutaḥ |
prāpnoti nirvāṇasukhaṃ śubhopayukto vā svargasukhaṃ || I 11 ||

The self that has developed equanimity, if endowed with pure activities, attains the bliss of Nirvāṇa, and if endowed with auspicious activities, attains heavenly happiness [tr. p. 385].

These examples suffice to show that in his celebrated philosophical work PraSā, Kundakunda uses the word *upayoga* in a different way from that found in Umāsvāti and also in the

Jaina canon. He does not discuss the term here with reference to *jñāna* and *darśana*, but rather in the general ethical sense of "pure" or "auspicious" activities and natures, which then lead to corresponding results, or their opposites. In his *Pañcāsti-kāya-sāra* (PaS), however, Kundakunda has three stanzas, 40–42, in which *upayoga* is used in the sense discussed above:

uvaogo khalu duviho ṇāṇeṇa ya daṃsaṇeṇa saṃjutto |
jīvassa savva-kālaṃ aṇaṇṇabhūdaṃ viyāṇīhi || 40 ||
upayogaḥ khalu dvi-vidho jñānena ca darśanena saṃyuktaḥ |
jīvasya sarva-kālam ananya-bhūtaṃ vijñānīhi || 40 ||

Upayoga is of two kinds, associated with *jñāna* and *darśana*.
Know it as always existing inseparably from the *jīva*.

ābhiṇisudodhimaṇa-kevalāṇi ṇāṇāni paṃca-bheyāṇi |
kumadi-suda-vibhaṃgāṇi ya tinni vi ṇāṇehi saṃjutte || 41
ābhinibodhika-śrutāvadhi-manaḥ-paryaya-kevalāni jñānāni pañca-bhedāni |
kumati-śruta-vibhaṅgāni ca trīṇy api jñānaiḥ saṃyuktāni || 41||

Ābhinibodhika [= *mati*], *śruta, avadhi, manaḥ-paryaya, kevala* are the five kinds which make up *jñāna*. These are connected with three further (kinds of) knowledge, *ku-mati, ku-śruta* and *vibhaṅga*.

daṃsaṇam avi cakkhu-judaṃ acakkhu-judam avi ya ohiṇā sahiyaṃ |
aṇidhaṇam aṇaṃta-visayaṃ kevaliyaṃ cāvi paṇṇattaṃ || 42 ||
darśanam api cak uryutam acak uryutam api cāvadhinā sahitaṃ |
anidhanam ananta-viṣayaṃ kaivalyaṃ cāpi prajñaptam || 42 ||

Darśana is what is connected to sight, to non-sight, (and) to *avadhi*.
Kaivalya, which is unlimited and eternal, is also so known.

The similarity between this and the list of eight kinds of *jñānopayogas* and four kinds of *darśanopayogas* in Pūjyapāda's commentary to TS 2, 9 mentioned above is evident. It would be interesting to know why Kundakunda deals with *upayoga* in such different ways in his two works discussed here. Further, Kundakunda does not seem to have dealt with the question of *upayoga* in the sense of *sākāra* and *anākāra* mentioned above.

Vidyānandin's commentary on Umāsvāti's TS is called *Tattvārtha-śloka-vārtika* and to TS 2, 9 (*sa dvividho 'ṣṭa-catur-bhedaḥ*), he says at the very beginning (p. 322 of the edition used here): *sa upayogo dvi-vidhas tāvat, sākāro jñānopayogaḥ saviśeṣārtha-viṣa-*

yatvāt, nirākāro darśanopayogaḥ sāmānya-viṣayatvāt | '*Upayoga* is indeed of two kinds: *jñānopayoga*, which is *sākāra* because it is restricted to an object possessing specific qualities, [and] *darśanopayoga* which is *nirākāra* because it is restricted to generality' (see e.g. pp. 35 and 38 above for *sākāra* and *nirākāra*). The rest of the commentary deals, among other things not directly relevant to the context here, with why the bigger number 'eight' appearing before the smaller number 'four' in the *sūtra* (saying that it is so decided in the *sūtra* because of its greater importance, *abhyarhitatvāt*). This means that in his basic understanding of *upayoga* Vidyānandin includes Pūjyapāda's views on the topic.

It was said above that the introduction of the terms *sākāra* and *anākāra* blurs the strict distinction between *upayoga* and *pramāṇa*. In trying to trace the development of these ideas in the canon, Kundakunda, Umāsvāti and Vidyānandin we saw that there are several issues about which hardly anything can be decided:

1. What lead to the change from the twofold distinction between *upayoga* and *paśyattā* in the canon to the later idea of one single term *upayoga* which is said to have a twofold division called *jñāna* and *darśana*? Or to put it another way, why was the term *paśyattā* abandoned, and the term *upayoga* used differently? Another alternative would be to ask the purely theoretical question: was there another overriding term in the canon under which rubric *upayoga* and *paśyattā* were included?

2. The terms *sākāra* and *anākāra* appear in the canon and the commentaries to TS 2, 9 use them as well, obviously in a sense different from the canon: the canon uses them with reference to *upayoga* and *paśyattā* both of which can be *sākāra* as well as *anākāra* (p. 5), whereas the commentaries to TS 2, 9 uses the term *upayoga* alone in the context of *jñāna* and *darśana*, in

which the former is *sākāra* and the latter *anākāra* (p. 35 above). Can one say that there probably was a phase, unbeknown to us, which led to this change in Jaina thinking? In a general way this question is related to the problem mentioned above in 1. Here the point is the unexplained adoption of the exact terms, albeit in another, and specific, context.

Although this chapter began with the presupposition that the concept of *upayoga* not only comes within the gamut of ontology but also epistemology (and ethics, as we saw in Kundakunda), in the light of what has been said above it seems now that this position either has to be revised or qualified. It would have to be revised because if identical terms are used in both ontology and epistemology their uses should apply in identical senses, and qualified because if this is not the case (as we saw above) then their uses would have be clearly delineated. This latter point is a legitimate problem because if one looks at the treatment of Jaina epistemology the occurrence or function also of *upayoga* in it is largely omitted, in any case not sufficiently emphasized in the light of the discussion above.[14] In this sense the treatment of epistemology will have to be revisited in the light of what has been dealt with above.

An attempt can now be made, in conclusion and on the basis of what has been said above, to try and answer the questions posed at the very outset of this chapter. The first one was: what are the *darśana* and *jñāna* functions exactly and do they take place simultaneously?

The Jaina canon speaks of *upayoga* and *paśyattā*, both of which can be *sākāra* as well as *anākāra*. We encountered the cryptic statement in the canon that since *jñāna* is *sākāra* and *darśana* is *anākāra*, no one can have *jñāna* and *darśana* simultaneously, neither a normal individual nor a *kevalin* (as seen above). We also saw that the later tradition abandoned the canonical distinction between *upayoga* and *paśyattā*, although

---

[14] See, e.g., Padmarajiah 1963, Shastri 1990, Soni 2000.

it retained the *sākāra/anākāra* division, but now under the general rubric of *upayoga*, which is said to be twofold, namely, *jñāna* and *darśana* (the former being *sākāra* and the latter *anākāra*). The term *paśyattā* was abandoned completely. This means that the *upayoga* and *paśyattā* of the canon are only of theoretical interest.

In the case of the TS with regard to the *darśana* and *jñāna* functions, a distinction has to be made between the *sūtras* themselves and the commentaries on them. We saw in TS 2, 8–9 that *upayoga* is the sign of consciousness and that it is of two kinds (*jñāna* and *darśana*) which in turn are of eight and four kinds, without these being enumerated individually in the *sūtra* itself (p. 35 above). Whereas the SS says that the two kinds of *upayoga* occur in succession in ordinary mortals (non-omniscients) and simultaneously in those who have annihilated karmas, the *Svopajña-bhāṣya* does not say anything about them in commenting on TS 2, 8–9.[15]

---

[15] However, TS 1, 30/31 gives a direct hint that certain kinds of knowledge can be had simultaneously: 'in a single soul, one, etc., up to four kinds (of knowledge) can be had simultaneously' (*ekādāni bhājyāni yugapad ekasminn ā caturbhyaḥ*). From the context it is clear that the reference is to four of the five kinds of knowledge mentioned in TS 1, 9 (*mati, śruta, avadhi, manaḥ-paryāya* and *kevala*; see also p. 35 and fn. 7 above). The simultaneity here cannot refer to *upayoga* but rather to the concurrency of the first four kinds, with *kevala* being given an independent status. This means that *mati* (sensory knowledge), *śruta* (scriptural knowledge), *avadhi* (clairvoyance), and *manaḥ-paryāya* (telepathy) can occur simultaneously in a single *jīva*. This simultaneity does not apply in the case of *kevala-jñāna* (omniscience or independent knowledge) in which there is no role of *mati*, etc. In their commentaries to 1, 30/31 the SS and the *Svopajña-bhāṣya* have a significant difference because the word *upayoga* appears only in the latter (p. 56 of the 1932 ed.): *mati-jñānādiṣu caturṣu paryāyeṇopayogo bhavati na yugapat* | *saṃbhinna-jñāna-darśanasya tu bhagavataḥ kevalino yugapat sarva-bhāva-grāhake nirapekṣe kevala-jñāne kevala-darśane cānusamayam upayogo bhavati* | Tatia 1951: 75, from where the reference is taken, translates this so: "The conscious activities manifesting themselves as *mati, śruta, avadhi* and *manaḥ-paryāya* occur in succession, and not simultaneously. The conscious activities of the omni-

In the case of Kundakunda we saw that he deals with *upayoga* in different ways in his two works discussed above on pp. 7–8 above. A clear statement about the occurrence of *jñāna* and *darśana* is given in his *Niyama-sāra* 159 where he says that: 'For a person who has *kevala-jñāna, jñāna* and *darśana* occur simultaneously, just as light and heat in the sun occur (simultaneously), so it is to be known.'[16] The implication is that for an ordinary individual without *kevala-jñāna* these would occur in sequence. Vidyānandin too holds the same view.

The other question posed at the outset was: if *jñāna* and *darśana* as *upayogas* take place in sequence, which function takes place first and what is its status in relation to the other? The position of the canon can be omitted here because its *upayoga/paśyattā* was abandoned. In the case of the TS the answer would have to be given on the basis of a clear distinction

---

scient lord, possessed of integrated *jñāna* and *darśana*, however, in respect of 'pure knowledge' and 'pure intuition' — which comprehend all objects and are independent — occur simultaneously in every point of time." The first mention of *upayoga* in the *sūtras* themselves is in TS 2, 8–9 (and said to be *darśana* and *jñāna* in the commentaries), so it is puzzling why the *Svopajña-bhāṣya* would mention the word *upayoga* in commenting on TS 1, 9 (the *darśana* and *jñāna* mentioned here is only in the context of *kevala-darśana* and *-jñāna* and not as *jñāno-* and *darśanopayoga*). Moreover, it seems quite logical that in ordinary cognition, for instance, sensory knowledge and scriptural knowledge could occur together — and this is what *sūtra* 1, 30/31 itself says, namely, that up to four kinds can occur together. Is there a contradiction or is it a matter of interpretation? In the light of the discussion here the problem could be solved if we apply what has been said here in *Svopajña-bhāṣya* 1, 31 to TS 2, 9. This would require a much more detailed analysis than can be done here. One further point can be noted here: in comparing the SS and the *Svopajña-bhāṣya* on the question of simultaneity of the two *upayogas darśana* and *jñāna* Tatia 1951: 75 contrasts them on the basis of the commentaries on different *sūtras*, namely, on 2, 9 and 1, 30/31 respectively.

[16] The Prakrit and Sanskrit texts are: *jugavaṃ vaṭṭai ṇāṇaṃ kevala-ṇānissa daṃsaṇaṃ ca tahā | diṇayara-payāsatāpaṃ jaha vaṭṭai taha muṇeyavvam || 159 || yugapad vartate jñānaṃ kevala-jñānino darśanaṃ ca tathā | dinakara-prakāśa-tāpau yathā vartete tathā jñātavyam || 159 ||*

between *darśana* and *jñāna*, where *jñāna* is described as knowledge (in the sense of cognition) which is 'with a form or is specific' (*sākāra*) and that *darśana* is cognition which is 'without a form or is unspecific' (*anākāra*). The commentaries to TS 2, 9, where these terms appear (see p. 35 above), explain in a Jaina way the general description in Indian epistemology between indeterminate perception (*nirvikalpaka-pratyakṣa*) and determinate perception (*savikalpaka-pratyakṣa*) where the former is the bare perception of an object of cognition (namely, that something is being cognised) and the latter the perception of the same object specifically in terms of its name and in terms of the class of things to which it may belong. The sequence of these two types of perception is logically from the indeterminate to the determinate, and in Jainism precisely this is the *anākāra/sākāra* distinction as it applies to *darśana /jñāna* as *upayogas*. In other words, *upayoga* has to be seen in two senses: one in its ontological sense as a sign of *caitanya* which is an intrinsic quality of the sentient principle (namely, that when it is embodied it has the condition for the possibility of implementing the function of knowing or cognising) and, secondly, the actual function as it occurs in human beings who are under the sway of *karman*, i.e., unenlightened beings. In this case the one cannot function without the other, that is, perception involves both an unspecific or formless (*anākāra*) cognition, followed by a cognition which is specific and with form (*sākāra*). As pointed out this distinction is not given in the TS itself, but rather in the commentaries.

The third question was whether *darśana* and *jñāna* as *upayogas* have separate identities, namely, whether each can operate without the function of the other. Obviously the answer is in the negative because cognition as such and as a whole undergoes these two stages. The question does not apply to *kevalins*, i.e. those who have *kevala-jñāna*, independent knowledge, because knowledge takes place independently of *mati*, *śruta*, etc. (see fn. 15 above).

The question was also asked: what is the precise difference between say *jñāna* as an *upayoga* and *jñāna* as a *pramāṇa*? The answer was implied in the discussion on p. 34 above where it was said that in the TS a clear distinction has to be made in the use of terms as they are used in specific *sūtras*, and their commentaries. In our case we highlighted the point that *darśana* and *jñāna* in TS 1, 1 are not used in the epistemological context of TS 1, 9. In the case of *upayoga*, TS 2, 8–9 and their commentaries were dealt with in detail in order to exemplify a further specific use of *jñāna* and *darśana*. The short answer to the inquiry in question is the obvious point that even if identical words are used, their contexts have to be analysed in detail, as was attempted above.

The gist of this last point hints at the question of the translation of terms. The problem was already indicated above. It is hoped that the following suggestions may be useful. When talking of *darśana* and *jñāna* in TS 1, 1 it would be appropriate to use their extensions in the context of the *sūtra*: *samyag-darśana* and *samyag-jñāna* (the third being *samyak-cāritra*) which are usually translated as proper faith, proper knowledge (and proper conduct) as factors which play the key role for those who follow the path to liberation, *mokṣa-mārga*, implying thereby that all three together constitute the path. The word *jñāna* in TS 1, 9 is perhaps best translated as a means or instrument of cognition, where *jñāna* would be a synonym for *pramāṇa* (TS1, 10 says that the five *mati*, etc., are *pramāṇas*), in the epistemological sense of the cognition (*pramā*) of what is to be known (*prameya*) through a specific means or instrument of cognition (*pramāṇa*). All these points then make up the theory of cognition (*prāmāṇya-vāda*). The key word *upayoga* could be translated as 'function', in the sense of what constitutes the 'sign' (*lakṣaṇa*) of consciousness (*caitanya*) which is an intrinsic component or quality (*guṇa*) of the sentient principle. Here 'function' would imply a 'faculty' or 'application' of the sentient principle, something that it is capable of applying, as its own sign. When *upayoga* takes place it indicates the existence or presence of consciousness. This would mean that here too, for the sake of clarity *darśana* and *jñāna* should be used in their extended forms of *darśanopayoga* and *jñānopayoga*. These in turn could be translated in terms of what the commentaries say, namely, as the function of unspecific or formless (*anākāra*) cognition, and the function of cognition which is specific and with form (*sākāra*). In short: *darśanopayoga* would be indeterminate or bare perception and *jñānopayoga* would be determinate or specific perception.[17]

[17] It has not been possible here to include several other thinkers in the Jaina tradition who have dealt with *upayoga* in a detailed manner. In the ongoing concern with the theme, it would be useful to pursue the study by analysing and comparing in detail the views, for example, of Siddhasena Divākara (*c.* fifth century, especially his *San-mati-tarka-prakaraṇa*) and Yaśo-vijaya (seventeenth century, especially his *Jñāna-bindu-prakaraṇa*). Malla-vādin's (fifth-sixth century) ideas would also be interesting because Yaśo-vijaya refers to him.

Chapter 4
Jaina *Khyāti-vāda* or Theory of Error

The main contents of this chapter were published in Soni 2012 under the title "Jaina Epistemology Revisited: On Erroneous Cognition". In Chapter 1 above in the Introduction, it was seen how the significance of epistemology was recognised from early times by almost all Indian thinkers, including within it the attempt to explain how error creeps into the process of our cognition of objects. As already pointed out he Indian tradition developed over time various theories of error, in accordance with the ontology and metaphysics of the tradition concerned. Cases of so-called error, such as the meeting of the sky and the earth in the horizon or absurd statements like the child of a barren woman, were not taken as seriously as the error in mistaking, for example, a rope for a snake, and the reaction of say the fear it can cause, to mention a well-known case. Cases of taking a rope for a snake do not always occur, as do the apparent meeting of the sky and the earth in the horizon. However, it was regarded as necessary to explain the occurrence of the error, when and if the reaction should occur on account of seeing a snake in the rope. In other words, a theory of valid cognition should also account for inevitable error that can occur in our cognition.

This chapter thus pays attention to the Jaina theory of error, which was hinted at above in the account concerning the term *upayoga*. In so doing it draws attention to the fact that erroneous cognition, signified by such terms as *maty-ajñāna*, *śrutājñāna* and *vibhaṅga-jñāna* (*avadhy-ajñāna*), is not an insignificant aspect in Jaina epistemology. *Tattvārtha-sūtra* 1,

31/32,[1] for example, says: *mati-śrutāvadhayo viparyayaś ca* ("sensory knowledge, knowledge of scripture and clairvoyance 'may also' be erroneous"). These three terms were earlier said to be means of valid cognition (TS 1, 9), and only later refers back to them saying that these three could also be erroneous. The context will be dealt with below in which these ideas about error are to be understood within the specific set of epistemological categories used in Jainism. In addition to the *sūtra* mentioned (TS 1, 31/32) recourse will be taken especially to TS 1, 9–12 where the epistemological categories are mentioned and to TS 2, 8–9 (especially to the two main commentaries on them) which refer to the technical term *upayoga* and its two kinds (*darśanopayoga* and *jñānopayoga*) for the context in which *maty-ajñāna*, etc. are used. Thus, this chapter pleads for the necessity of explicitly mentioning *maty-ajñāna*, etc., as significant for the understanding of Jaina epistemology as a whole and including this aspect, especially since standard works on the theme either ignore them, or do not sufficiently emphasise their importance.

The theory of cognition (*prāmāṇyavāda*) in Indian philosophy is a topic that has taken the centre-stage practically from the earliest times of philosophical activity[2] and the Jainas have not lagged behind in making their own contribution.[3] The words *pramā/pramiti*, *prameya*, *pramāṇa* and *pramātṛ* etymologically belong to the topic insofar as they respectively refer to cognition, the object of cognition, the means of cognition (like

---

[1] The number after the stroke refers to the *sūtra* in the Śvetāmbara version of the TS.

[2] See, for example, Dasgupta 1932: 378–388 on epistemological terms in the *Carakasaṃhitā*; also in Frauwallner: 1994: 66–86. See Datta 1960 for the "six ways of knowing in Vedānta", mentioned in Chapter 1 above.

[3] Some general studies on Jaina epistemology are, for example: Padmarajiah 1963, Dixit 1971 (p. 22, for instance, has a section with the title "Evolution of the treatment of Pramāṇa", apart from other individual sections), Shastri 1990, Bhattacharyya 1994. See also fn. 6 below.

perception and inference), and the subject of cognition (that is, the one who cognises). In this context the question of using the word knowledge (*jñāna*) as a synonym for cognition (*pramā/pramiti*), as in *pratyakṣa-jñāna*, is an important one when speaking of *prāmāṇyavāda*. The problem has not been unnoticed and for our purposes we can regard it "as an instance of loose thinking".[4] It seems that it is the context which determines whether *jñāna* may be taken as a synonym for *pramā/pramiti*, without leading to any major problems in understanding the meaning of the point made when either or both terms are used.

In Indian thought theories of error are implicit in the concern with epistemology, based perhaps on the presupposition that human cognition/knowledge can also be fallible, and thus needed to be accounted for. In other words, taking into account the generally accepted possibility of human fallibility, Indian thinkers not only acknowledge this fact, but they also sought to explain this phenomenon. The question to which an answer was sought is: how does the occurrence of error fit into the structure of the human process of cognition? The question is significant because for the *ātma-vādins*, for example, the self, or the *ātman*, intrinsically possesses know-

---

[4] Datta 1960: 19 speaking about *jñāna* and *pramā* says:"Consequently knowledge, strictly speaking, should always stand for a cognition that is true, uncontradicted and unfalsified. The ordinary division of knowledge into true knowledge and false knowledge should, therefore, be considered *as an instance of loose thinking;* the word true as applied to knowledge would then be a tautology, and the word false positively contradictory—false knowledge being only a name for falsified knowledge, which is another name for no knowledge" (my emphasis). On *cetanā*, *buddhi*, *jñāna* and *saṃvit* see, for example, Bhatt 1989: 55–57. Since experience (*anubhava*) plays an important role for the goal to be achieved in Indian philosophy, as contrasted with mere description (*lakṣaṇa*), a distinction can be drawn between 'cognition-experience' and 'knowledge-experience' when dealing with *prāmāṇya-vāda*. For this in the context of Śaiva Siddhānta philosophy see Soni 1989: 100.

ledge (this would apply to Jaina philosophy as well insofar as the *jīva* can in a certain sense be seen as *ātman*, namely as the principle of sentience which makes cognition at all possible). It is this point about the occurrence of error which has led Indian thinkers to propound several theories of error (*khyāti-vāda*).[5]

When (and if) the occurrence of error is dealt with in a basic treatment of Jaina epistemology then it is either in very general terms or dismissed with very briefly.[6] The reason for this might simply be that the topic has not roused much interest in the case of Jainism. In the *Tattvārthasūtra*[7] (TS, *c.*

[5] As mentioned in Chapter 1 above, the 'realistic' theories of error are *akhyāti-vāda* and *anyathā-khyāti-vāda*. The 'idealistic' one are *ātma-khyāti-vāda*, *asat-khyāti-vāda* and *anirvacanīya-khyāti-vāda*. For brief details see also Soni 1989: 165. It seems that jut as theories of error in Indian philosophy do not receive adequate treatment when dealing with epistemology in general, the same holds true for Western philosophy, to judge, for example, from the statement: "Many contemporary philosophers rate error theories poorly" (Chris Daly and David Liggins 2010: 209). The context of these error theories is certainly different, because, for example Daly and Liggins suggest that "there are exactly two fundamental sources of knowledge: perception and thought" (224–225), whereas for classical Indian philosophy six sources are discussed (as in Vedānta). If "thought" could be seen as a synonym for inference (*anumāna*) then they may be sufficient grounds for a fruitful comparative study, especially when one reads such statements as: "Given any putative source of evidence *S* for a proposition *P*, an error theory about *P* may either dispute whether *S* is a source of evidence, or it may claim that *S*'s evidential support for *P* is defeated by the counter-evidence that the error theory marshals" (225).

[6] See Shastri 1990: 463–464, for example, albeit under the chapter dealing with *ajñāna*, ignorance. The pages referred to here are under the section "The Cause of Wrong Knowledge". Padmarajiah 1963 and Soni 2000 who also deal with the basics of Jaina epistemology do not have anything significant to say about erroneous knowledge/cognition. See also fn. 3 above.

[7] The translations used below are based on Jain 1992 and the Sanskrit text is quoted from the 1955 edition of Pūjyapāda's *Savārtha-siddhi* (SS), regarded by the Digambaras to be the first commentary on the TS. The Śvetāmbaras say that Umāsvāti wrote an auto-commentary, the *Svopajña-bhāṣya*; quotations from it are from the 1932 ed. given under Umāsvāti.

fifth-century CE) by the Jaina thinker Umāsvāmin/Umāsvāti, written in the *sūtra* style of the other systems of Indian philosophy—the fundamental and first Sanskrit work for basic Jaina philosophy—the reference to erroneous knowledge appears briefly (in fact in only two *sūtras* given below), long after the basic facts of Jaina epistemology are given in TS 1, 9–12, where each of the *pramāṇas* is described in *sūtra* format; the mention of possible error first appears in TS 31/32 and 1, 32/33[8]. For the context of the topic of this chapter it is useful to first repeat what the text says in TS 1, 9–12:

> *mati-śrutāvadhi-manaḥ-paryāya-kevalāni jñānam* 1, 9: Sensory knowledge, knowledge of scripture, clairvoyance, telepathy and omniscience [these five together yield] knowledge.
>
> *tat-pramāṇe* 1, 10: These [five] are the two *pramāṇas* [*parokṣa* and *pratyakṣa*].
>
> *ādye parokṣam* 1, 11: The first two [*mati* and *śruta*] are indirect (*pramāṇas*).
>
> *pratyakṣam anyat* 1, 12; The others are direct (*pramāṇas*) [namely the other three: *avadhi*, *manaḥ-paryāya* and *kevali*] .

As is well-known, not only is the distinction between *parokṣa* and *pratyakṣa* unique to Jainism, but also the various means of cognition or knowledge listed under them and described in TS 1, 13–30/31. TS 1, 31/32 explicitly mentions error (*viparyaya*) for the first time, with TS 32/33 immediately supplying the reason why knowledge could be erroneous:

> *mati-śrutāvadhayo viparyayaś ca* (TS 1, 31/32), *sad-asator aviśeṣād yadṛcchopalabdher unmatta-vat* (TS 1, 32/33).
>
> Sensory knowledge, knowledge of scripture, clairvoyance also are [or: can be] erroneous; on account of not distinguishing between the real and the unreal, knowledge (*upalabdhi*) is [can be] accidental, like that of a lunatic/drunkard.

It may be noted that in terms of the classification of means of cognition/knowledge into the two types given in TS 1, 11–12, the first two, *mati* and *śruta*, are *parokṣa*, indirect means,

---

[8] See fn. 1 above.

and the third, *avadhi,* is *pratyakṣa* or the direct means. In the context of error that can occur through them, it is insignificant whether the means in question is indirect or direct. What is important is the outcome, the (false) cognition/knowledge that can result. Our task now is to analyse these statements in order to understand what the Jaina point here would be. The best starting point for this is to see what the commentaries to these *sūtras* say.

Sarvārtha-siddhi (SS) on TS 1, 31/32:

> *viparyayo mithyety arthaḥ* । *kutaḥ ? samyag-adhikārāt* । *'ca' śabdaḥ samuccayārthaḥ* । *viparyayaś ca samyañceti kutaḥ punar eṣāṃ viparyayaḥ ? mithyā-darśanena sahaikārtha-samavāyāt sa-rajas-kakaṭukālābu-gata-dugdha-vat* । *nanu ca tatrādhāra-doṣād dugdhasya rasa-viparyayo bhavati* । *na ca tathā maty-ajñānādināṃ viṣaya-grahaṇe viparyayaḥ* । *tathā hi, samyag-dṛṣṭir yathā cakṣur ādibhī rūpādīn upalabhate tathā mithyā-dṛṣṭir api maty-ajñānena* । *yathā ca samyg-dṛṣṭiḥ śrutena rūpādīn jānāti nirūpayati ca tathā mithyā-dṛṣṭir api śrutājñānena* । *yathā cāvadhi-jñānena samyag-dṛṣṭiḥ rūpiṇo 'rthān avagacchati tathā mithyā-dṛṣṭir vibhaṅga-jñāneneti* ।
>
> Error [here in the *sūtra*] has the meaning [what is cognised] 'incorrectly'/'wrongly'. [Objection:] How [can this be], because the topic is about [what is] right/correct.[9] [Reply:] The word '*ca*' has the meaning of conjunction.[10] [Objection:] Again, how are/can these be in error? [Reply: this happens] because of the co-inherence with synonymity [with what is wrong and what is right in the *jīva*] through false belief, like milk turns bad (*kaṭuka*) in a pumpkin gourd (*ālābu*) with impurity. [Objection:] On account of the fault there in the container, there is a change/error (*viparyaya*) in the fluid of the milk. In the same way (*tathā*) there cannot be a change when *maty-ajñāna,*

---

[9] The reference is not only to TS 1, 1: *samyag-darśana-jñāna-cāritrāṇi mokṣa-mārgaḥ* । 'Right faith, right knowledge and right conduct [together] are the path to liberation', but also to the section here dealing with *pramāṇa,* (TS 1, 10: *tat-pramāṇe*) which is generally regarded as what is the source of valid/correct knowledge or cognition.

[10] The meaning would be that *mati, śruta* and *avadhi* are indeed valid means of knowledge, as said in TS 1, 9. TS 1, 31/32 now says that these are also, in the sense of 'can also be', in error at the same time. It is interesting to note that this statement coming after so many *sūtras* leads to another, and more qualified, understanding of TS 1, 9.

> etc. grasp an object [of cognition]. [Reply:] It is in the same way; just as the right view perceives form, etc., through the eyes and so on, so too also the wrong view through *maty-ajñāna* (non-sensory knowledge). Just as the right view knows and perceives form, etc., through *śruta* (knowledge of scripture), so too also the wrong view through *śrutājñāna* (non-knowledge of scripture). And just as the right view understands the meanings of forms, so too the wrong view through knowledge that is a fraud/deception.

It is noteworthy that this *sūtra* and its commentary come towards the end of the description of basic Jaina epistemology —noteworthy because they refer back to TS 1, 9 which now has to be understood with the qualifications expressed here. It is indeed unusual to refer to certain means of cognition/ knowledge as *pramāṇa* and then to say, later, that these very means *may* not be valid means of knowledge. The point of this *sūtra* and its commentary is that the *pramāṇas* in question should be seen as *having the possibility* of being in error as well, apart from the obvious possibility of being valid means. The *sūtra* itself does not hint at this interpretation and the sense of the verb that has to be supplied to it would have to be taken from the commentary. That is why the interpretation is not that the means *are* in error, but that they *could be, might also be* so, in other words the cognition/knowledge they yield could be both valid and invalid.[11] This would further have to be understood as meaning that only upon assessing their conclusions can one say whether the result is valid or not. These means err because of *mithyā-darśana* and/or *mithyā-dṛṣṭi*, as the commentary says. We shall return to this point in order to discuss how the error/falsity is to be decided upon.

The question could be asked whether the possibility of the fallibility of the *pramāṇas* mentioned here in TS 1, 31/32 could not have been included together with the *pramāṇas* in question when they were first listed in TS 1, 9, at least in the

---

[11] See Tatia 1994: 23. His translation of TS 1, 31/32 is: "Empirical, articulate and clairvoyant knowledge may be enlightened as well as deluded".

commentaries. This point will also be taken up below. Here, in elaborating the *sūtra*, the commentator explicitly mentions *maty-ajñāna*, *śrutājñāna* and *vibhaṅga-jñāna* (a synonym for *avadhy-ajñāna*); that is, *mati*, *śruta* and *avadhi* are non-knowledge, erroneous cognition (*ajñāna*), which I have rendered as non-sensory knowledge, non-knowledge of scripture and the last would be non-clairvoyance. The point of the analogy of milk becoming bad in a dirty gourd is that when *ajñāna* (non-knowledge) is present, when it dirties correct cognition/knowledge, the result is error; without *ajñāna* the same means would function validly. Let us now turn the Śvetāmbara commentary on this *sūtra*.

The *Svopajña-bhāṣya* on TS 1, 31/32:

> *mati-jñānaṃ śruta-jñānam avadhi-jñānam iti viparyayaś ca bhavaty ajñānaṃ cety arthaḥ । jñāna-viparyayo 'jñānam iti । atrāha । tad eva jñānaṃ tad evājñānam iti । nanu cchāyātapa-vac-chītoṣṇavac ca tad-atyanta-viruddham iti । atrocyate । — mithyādarśana-parigrahād viparīta-grāhakatvam eteṣām । tasmād ajñānāni bhavanti । tad yathā । — maty-ajñānaṃ śrutājñānaṃ vibhaṅgaj-ñānam iti । avadhir viparīto vibhaṅga ity ucyate ।*

> Sensory knowledge, knowledge of scripture, clairvoyance [with regard to these three] there is [or: can be] error also, this means [they lead to] non-knowledge. An error in knowledge is non-knowledge. Here an objector says: this very knowledge is non-knowledge! Like shade and sunshine (*ātapa*), cold and heat these (knowledge and non-knowledge) are absolutely contrary. To this (*atra*) we reply: on account of comprehending [the object of knowledge] through false belief these (means of knowledge) grasp erroneously, that is why they are non-knowledge. That is to say [they lead to]: non-sensory-knowledge, non-knowledge of scripture, non-clairvoyance. Clairvoyance that is an error is said to be a fraud/deception.

The *Svopajña-bhāṣya* on TS 1, 31/32 continued:

> *atrāha—uktaṃ bhavatā samyag-darśana-parigṛhītaṃ maty-ādi-jñānaṃ bhavaty anyathā 'jñānam eva iti । mithyā-dṛṣṭayo 'pi ca bhavyāś cābhavyāś cendriyanimittān aviparītān sparśādīn upalabhante, upadiśanti ca sparśaṃ sparśa iti rasaṃ rasa iti, evaṃ śeṣān । tat katham etad iti । atrocyate । — teṣāṃ hi viparītam etad bhavati ।*

> You said, Sir, [an object of knowledge] grasped through right belief is sensory knowledge, etc., otherwise/erroneously (*anyathā*) it is non-knowledge. Even in the case of a wrong view, touch, etc., under the influence of the senses, be they proper or not (*bhavyāś cābhavyās*), perceive without error, and indicate touch as touch, taste as taste, in the same way the rest [of the senses]. How is this so? Here we reply: there is error here with these [means of knowledge].

These two parts of the Śvetāmbara commentary on TS 1, 31/32 say in essence the same thing about the basic problem as the Digambara SS commentary on it: both begin by mentioning the problem of referring to *mati*, *śruta* and *avadhi* first as *jñāna* in TS 1, 9 and now in TS 31/32 as *viparyaya*, as being in error also—namely, that they could be *ajñāna*—leading to a contradiction of terms with regard to the same means of cognition/knowledge. The Śvetāmbara commentary refers to an objector who says that this is as contradictory as shade/sunshine and cold/heat. The reason for the error in both commentaries, is attributed to *maty-ajñāna*, *śrutājñāna* and *vibhaṅga-jñāna* (*avadhy-ajñāna*). As already mentioned the SS commentary, explains on the analogy of milk turning bad through the impurity in the vessel in which it is stored, leads to cognition/knowledge 'turning bad'.

At the end of the commentary on TS 1, 31/32, the *Svopajña-bhāṣya* has no link to the next *sūtra*, TS 1, 32/33. The SS commentary on the other hand says *atrocyate*, "here [with regard to the reason why *mati*, etc., could err] the *sūtra-kāra* says" (re-quoted from above):

> *sad-asator aviśeṣād yadṛcchopalabdher unmatta-vat* (TS 1, 32/33): "On account of not distinguishing between the real and the unreal, knowledge (*upalabdhi*) is [or can be] accidental, like that of a lunatic/drunkard".

The SS on TS 1, 32/33:

> *sad vidyamānam asad avidyamānam ity arthaḥ | tayor aviśeṣeṇa yadṛc-chayā upalabdher viparyayo bhavati | kadā cid rūpādisad apy asad iti pratipadyate, asad api sad iti, kadā cit sat sad eva, asad apy asad eveti mithyā-darśanodayād adhyavasyati | yathā pittodayākulita-buddhir māta-*

raṃ bhāryeti, bhāryām api māteti manyate | yadṛcchayā yadāpi mātaraṃ mātaiveti bhāryam api bhāryaiveti ca tadāpi na tat samyag-jñānam ~evaṃ matyādināṃ rūpādiṣu viparyayo veditavyaḥ | tathā hi, kaścin mithyā-darśana-pariṇāma ātmany avasthito rūpādy-upalabdhau satyām api kāraṇa-viparyāsaṃ bhedābheda-viparyāsaṃ svarūpaviparyāsaṃ ca janayati | ...[12]*| tatas tan-maty-ajñānaṃ śrutajñānaṃ vibhaṅga-jñānaṃ ca bhavati | samyag-darśanaṃ punas tattvārthādhigame śraddhānam utpādayati | tatas tan-mati-jñānaṃ śruta-jñānam avadhi-jñānaṃ ca bhavati |*

Sat is [what is] real and *asat* [what is] unreal, is the meaning [of the words in the *sūtra*]. There is error in both because the cognition/ knowledge (*upalabdhi*) is by chance, since it is without distinction [between what is real and what is not]. Sometimes, as a consequence of wrong belief *(mithyā-darśana)*, it [the cognition/knowledge] regards form, etc., even if they are real, to be unreal, [and] even if they are unreal to be real; sometimes it considers the real as real, even the unreal as unreal: like [for instance regarding] the mother as the wife through a bewildered/perplexed mind as a consequence of [the ill-effect of] bile [and sometimes] considers even the wife as the mother. Sometimes although by chance/accident it regards the mother as the mother and the wife as the wife, then this to is [strictly speaking] not right knowledge. In this way, the error of sensory knowledge, etc. [namely, of *śruta* and *avadhi* as well] is to be understood with regard to [a cognition/knowledge of] form, etc. That is to say, the transformation which takes place *(avasthita)* in a person on account of wrong belief gives rise to a mistake with regard to the cause, a mistake with regard to difference and identity and a mistake in the intrinsic nature [of an object], even when there is a cognition of form, etc. ... Thus, there is in these non-sensory knowledge, non-knowledge of scripture and non-clairvoyance. Right belief, on the other hand, produces conviction in the knowledge *(adhigame)* of things in reality. Thus there is in this [valid] sensory knowledge, knowledge of scripture and clairvoyance.

The key factor, then, in the Jaina theory of erroneous

[12] About nine lines of the ed. used here have been omitted, in which the three kinds of error (with regard to the cause, difference and identity, and nature of the object of cognition/knowledge), are elaborated with reference to some *(kecit)* views which are not accepted by the Jainas because they are opposed to what is known through perception and inference *(dṛṣṭeṣṭa-viruddhāt)*. These errors come about as a consequence of wrong belief (*mithyā-darśanodayāt*).

cognition/knowledge is wrong belief *(mithyā-darśana)*, which the SS contrasts with right belief (*samyag-darśana)*. Wrong belief leads to a cognition of an object such that it is seen as what it is not. It does not matter whether the object, by fluke, is seen as it really is, if wrong belief is responsible for it. The obvious question is how does one know that this is the case, that wrong belief is the responsible factor? The answer becomes complex because it involves a discussion of what right belief is, a term which takes us back to TS 1, 1 for its specific Jaina significance. Before entering into this discussion, let us see what the *Svopajña-bhāṣya* has to say on this TS 1, 32/33.

The *Svopajña-bhāṣya* on TS 1, 32/33:

> *yathonmattaḥ karmodayād upahatendriya-matir viparīta-grāhī bhavati* I *so 'śvaṃ gaur ity adhyavasyati gāṃ cāśva iti loṣṭaṃ suvarṇam iti suvarṇaṃ loṣṭa iti loṣṭaṃ ca loṣṭa iti suvarṇaṃ suvarṇam iti tasyaivam aviśeṣeṇa loṣṭaṃ suvarṇaṃ suvarṇaṃ loṣṭam iti viparītam adhyavasyato niyatam ajñānam eva bhavati* I *tadvan mithyā-darśenopahatendriya-mater mati-śrutāvadhayo 'py ajñānaṃ bhavanti* I
>
> Just as: a lunatic/drunkard whose sensory cognition/knowledge is seduced as a consequence of karma, grasps [an object of cognition] wrongly—he considers a horse to be a cow and the cow a horse, a lump of earth gold and gold a lump of earth, a lump of earth a lump of earth, gold gold, without distinction, the wrong consideration that a lump of earth is gold, gold a lump of earth, is certainly non-knowledge—so too, because of the opinion that the sense organs are seduced by wrong belief, even sensory knowledge, knowledge of scripture and clairvoyance are [in fact] non-knowledge.

This commentary gives a direct hint with regard to the point just mentioned about how right belief (*samyag-darśana*) becomes wrong *(mithyā-darśana*), namely, as a consequence of karma. In the context of the discussion here the reference is specifically to the *ghātiyā* karmas "which have a directly negative effect on the qualities of the *jīva*" and "are divided into four groups on the basis of which *jīva*-quality they affect; thus we have perception-obscuring (*darśanāvaraṇīya*), knowledge-obscuring (*jñānāvaraṇīya*), energy-obstructing (*vīryāntarāya*), and bliss-defiling (*mohanīya*) karmas" (Jaini 1979: 115). In addition to this, that is so as a result of the negative effects of the different types of karma, the *jīva's* quality states (*guṇa-sthānas*) are affected in its journey of purification, of ridding itself of all karmas. There are fourteen quality states of the *jīva* and by way of example only the first may be mentioned here for a better understanding not only of the complexity behind the Jaina theory of errors, but also for the context of what is intended in the commentaries quoted above: "1. *Mithyādṛṣṭi*: The lowest state, in which the soul suffers from "wrong views" (*mithyā-darśana)* because of the presence of *darśana-mohanīya* karmas and the *anantānubandhī* type of passions (*kaṣāya*)" (Jaini 1979, p. 272).

We postponed above two points for discussion: 1. how the error/falsity is to be decided upon and 2. the question whether the possibility of the fallibility of the *pramāṇas* mentioned in T S 1, 31/32 could not have been included together with the *pramāṇas* in question when they were first listed in TS 1, 9, at least in the commentaries.

The answer to first question can be regarded as being implicit in the reference above to the Jaina theory of karma and the associated quality states of the *jīva*. Obviously, if *mati*, *śruta* and *avadhi* lead to a knowledge that is not in keeping with the Jaina view of reality as contained in its canonical (Āgama) and pro-canonical works (like the TS itself), these means of cognition/knowledge would be seen as erroneous. This answer is not adequate because the fundamental problem remains: how is the basic Jaina view to be interpreted if there are differences of opinion not only among the different Jaina groups, like the Digambaras and Śvetāmbaras, but vis-à-vis non-Jaina views? Although this problem does not concern us here, it may be said that in terms of basic Jaina philosophy the TS is an authoritative work for both the Jaina traditions and that "their respective versions of this work show predictable disagreement on such controversial matters as the nudity of the mendicant and the partaking of food by the *kevalin*" (Jaini 1979: 82). In the examples of the two commentaries quoted above, we saw that the basic view in both is "almost identical" (to quote Jaini again from the same place when he speaks generally about the two TS versions and their commentaries).

The other part of the answer to the question about error/falsity concerns its position when compared with non-Jaina views. Here the problem would be more easily solved because, on the one hand, the Jaina could 'integrate' the opponents' views within its theory of manifoldness (*anekānta-vāda*) and regard them accordingly as being partially valid and, on the other hand, highlight the differences, for example, in terms of its own ontology, metaphysics and epistemology.

The second question about the fallibility of the *pramāṇas* mentioned in TS 1, 31/32 being included together with the *pramāṇas* when they were first listed in TS 1, 9 can be simply answered by saying that this is how the text has it and there can be no further discussion on the matter. However, it is certainly of academic interest because of the unusual nature, as already mentioned, of referring to certain means of cognition/knowledge as *pramāṇa* and then to say later that these very means *may* also be invalid. We saw the objection at the very beginning of the SS commentary on TS 1, 31/32 asking how it can be that these *pramāṇas* can err because the topic under discussion is about what is right/correct (referring to *samyag-darśana*, etc., and to *pramāṇa* as basically being what is valid). This indicates that the commentary seems to be aware of the problem. The fact that TS 1, 31/32 leads to a qualified interpretation TS 1, 9 (see fn. 9 above), to repeat, raises the question as to why this was not done in the first place. It may be suggested that the reason is to keep the two aspects separate: *mati*, *śruta* and *avadhi* belong to the list of *pramāṇas* listed in TS 1, 9–12 and that because of the commentaries to TS 2, 8–9 new aspects are introduced which not only refer to the earlier *sūtras* under discussion but list *maty-ajñāna*, *śrutājñāna* and *vibhaṅgājñāna* (*avadhy-ajñāna*) as three of the eight kinds of *jñānopayoga*.

These two *sūtras*, TS 2, 8–9, are cryptically short in the usual *sūtra* format: *upayogo lakṣaṇam* and *sa dvividho 'ṣṭa-catur-bhedaḥ*, *upayoga* is the 'sign' [of the *jīva*] and it [*upayoga*] is of two kinds [*jñānopayoga* and *darśanopayoga*, and these in turn are respectively of eight and four kinds. As just said, *mati*, etc., as *ajñāna* are three of eight kinds of *jñānopayoga*.

The new aspect of *upayoga* and the various types of *pramāṇas* listed under it broaden the scope of the Jaina theory of error. In addition to TS 1, 31/32, TS 2, 8–9 also draw our attention back to the *sūtras* at the beginning of the text when the *pramāṇas* are first dealt with, and the question about their now different understanding would apply in this case again. The context of TS 2, 8–9 is the nature of the *jīva* in which the actions or functions of *upayoga* as *jñānopayoga* and *darśanopayoga* (determinate or specific perception and indeterminate or bare perception respectively) are mentioned in the commentaries to them. This aspect has been investigated in the previous chapter on *upayoga* and further evinces the complexity of Jaina epistemology hinted at here.

It may be said that the significance of the Jaina theory of error rests on the direct relevance of TS 2, 8–9 for what was said in the first chapter of the TS at two places: TS 1, 9 which list the five means of cognition/knowledge, like *mati*, etc., and TS 1, 31/32 which state the first three could also be erroneous. The commentaries to TS 2, 8–9 then combine all the eight '*pramāṇas*', and show that three of the eight kinds could err. The *sūtras* TS 2, 8–9 themselves speak only of *upayoga* and its two kinds, *jñāna* and *darśana*. Only the commentaries to them mention the eight kinds in detail.

Precisely this elaboration of the eight kinds of '*pramāṇas*' has been attempted above which makes up the Jaina theory of error.

It may be asked, finally: how can the Jaina theory of error be classified in terms of those mentioned in chapter 1? It seems to be obvious in Jainism that an object is seen *as it is not* and therefore the Jaina theory of error is the cognition of an object as 'otherwise', namely as other than what it is in fact. Hence the Jaina theory of error is of the type called *anyathā-khyāti-vāda*. This is also attested by Hemacandra (eleventh century) when he says in his *Pramāna-mīmāṃsā* (1, 1, 7) that error "is a cognition which definitely takes a thing to be what it is not" (see Shah 2002: 63).

Chapter 5
Summary and Conclusion

The main contents of this chapter were published in Soni 2015a under the title "A Sketch of Jaina Epistemology".[1] Its main purpose was to try and show how Jainism not only has its own unique theory of knowledge (*prāmāṇya-vāda*), as is quite well-known, but also that in keeping with the Indian occupation with epistemology itself, it has its own theory of error (*khyāti-vāda*) as well.[2] Explaining how errors occur in human cognition was included in the epistemological theories and it is not often noticed that Indian epistemology dealt with theories of error as well. Indeed, as already stated, the success of a theory of valid cognition is commensurate with the success in which error in our cognition is also explained. In other words, granted that we can err in our cognition a theory of cognition should also be able to explain the source of this occurrence, or at least be in a position to account for its occurrence, as has already been noted a few times. Most standard presentations of basic Jain epistemology ignore this aspect, if they at all mention how the condition of the possibility of error can be explained in Jainism, as mentioned several times in the course of this study. When (and if) the occurrence of error is dealt with in a basic treatment of Jaina epistemology then it is either in very general terms or dismissed with very briefly.

---

[1] This printed version was based on a lecture at the kind invitation of Svastiśrī Cārukīrthi Bhaṭṭāraka Svamijī of Shravana Belagola that I gave in February 2015. His presence graced the occasion and I thank him profoundly for the honour and privilege concurred upon me.

[2] See the previous chapter.

The reason for this absence might simply be that the topic has not roused much interest in the case of Jainism. This chapter now attempts, by way of summarising what has already been said, to place again this particular aspect in proper perspective and context, and summarily combines previous work on it which, as pointed out, were independent studies; the basic ideas mentioned in what has been dealt with so far in this booklet are now put together here.

The themes already elaborated in the previous chapters, namely *dravya, guṇa* and *paryāya*, *upayoga* and *kyāti-vāda* have been dealt with with specific reference to their epistemological significance. What emerged as outcome is that a comprehensive treatment of Jaina epistemology cannot avoid the complexities contained in it. At least the following aspects belong to its core:

1. The basic means or instruments of knowledge. Standard works on Jaina epistemology usually begin and end with the five basic types divided into direct and indirect cognition, without the theory of error clearly traceable there.
2. The concept of substance with its quality and mode or modification and how this specifically applies to *both* the two basic substances in Jainism, namely *jīva* and *ajīva*. Both these substances are the players in the epistemological process regarding the object to be known *(prameya),* the subject that knows (*pramātṛ*) and the means through which the object is known (*pramāṇa*). Jaina epistemology is incomplete without the reference to the substances, their qualities and modes or modifications, particularly of the *jīva*-substance where the cognition takes place.
3. The exact reference to the means or instruments of cognition which can or may be erroneous has to be made more explicit because they cannot be avoided or ignored when dealing with Jaina epistemology.

All these points belong together in Jaina epistemology, giving it its due complexity.

It may be added that a fine-tuning of Jaina epistemology can be achieved by also taking recourse to the karma theory, particularly to the role of the *āvaraṇīya-karmas*, and the rung of the 'quality state' (*guṇa-sthāna*) reached in the fourteen runged ladder, depending on the elimination of the effects of a particular karma and the consequent knowledge obtained, as pointed out in the previous chapter. The theory of error explains how the knowledge can also be wrong or false because of the influence and effect of a particular karma. Moreover, the well-known *anekānta-vāda* with its two aspects of *syād-vāda* and *naya-vāda* add interesting aspects to Jaina epistemology, because of their fundamental attitude that our knowledge or cognition is always partial, that is, not 'completely' valid. The three chapters 2–4 summarised the main contents of this study.

The crux of the matter is that in Jainism knowledge or valid cognition takes place in the *jīva* itself, because it is the sentient principle and all activity is ultimately traceable back to it as the source. However, as is known, each *jīva* carries its own load of karma which can negatively affect it in its function(s), particularly when it comes to knowing or cognising.

In short, Jaina epistemology requires a detailed concern with TS 1, 9 (where the five *pramāṇas* are mentioned), TS 1, 31/32 (where it is said that three of the five can be erroneous) and TS 2, 8–9 (which deal with *upayoga* and its direct role in the epistemological activity).

In concluding this brief sketch let us briefly return to the point about *upayoga* being of two kinds, knowledge (*jñānopayoga*) and perception (*darśanopayoga*). What is interesting in the passage quoted above, p. 35, are the terms 'wrong sensory knowledge' (*maty-ajñāna*), 'wrong scriptural knowledge' (*śrutājñāna*) and 'wrong clairvoyance' (*vibhaṅga-jñāna/avadhy-ajñāna*). In most treatments of Jaina epistemology these terms are usually ignored, although they form a significant part of how we know what we know, in the case here also knowing wrongly. The reason for ignoring them is most probably because TS 1, 9 deals with the *pramāṇas* and the role of *upayoga* tends to get left out because it is discussed much later, in TS 2, 9. Pūjyapāda's commentary hints at the point that in fact we need to go back and see TS 1, 9 in the light of TS 2, 9.

TS 2, 9 accommodates the condition for the possibility of error as an intrinsic function of *jñāna* so as to account for probable cases of incorrect apprehension and false insights of the basic Jaina tenets, despite the fact that one follows the Jaina principles. The possibility of the occurrence of error is finally traced back to the notion of concealing karmas (*āvaraṇīya-karma*) of *jīva*. In other words, the function of *upayoga* in its manifestation as *jñāna* or knowledge is always obscured by karma in the case of beings not liberated from its influence, hence accounting for the condition of the possibility of error. Here it may only be pointed out that, as with the epistemology of other schools of Indian philosophy, the Jainas too have a theory of error. In other words, a theory of knowledge should also be able to account for the source of error in our cognition and knowledge. The question about how the error is finally resolved is a difficult one. It seems that the 'correct' view will depend upon a specific tradition which interprets the basic Jaina teaching in a specific way.

Finally, the question was asked about classifying the Jaina theory of error in terms of those mentioned in chapter one. It seemed obvious in Jainism that an object is seen as it is *not* and therefore the Jaina theory of error is the cognition of an object as 'otherwise', namely as other than what it is in fact. Hence the Jaina theory of error is of the type called *anyathā-khyāti-vāda*. This is also attested by Hemacandra (eleventh century) when he says in his *Pramāna-mīmāṃsā* (1, 1, 7) that error "is a cognition which definitely takes a thing to be what it is not" (see Shah 2002: 63).

Abbreviations and Literature

Balcerowicz, Piotr, 2001. *Jaina Epistemology in Historical Perspective. Critical Edition and English Translation of Logical-Epistemological Treatises: Nyāyâvatāra, Nyāyâvatāra-vivṛti and Nyāyâvatāra-ṭippana with Introduction and Notes*. In 2 volumes, Stuttgart: Steiner, 2001.

Bhargava, Dayanand,1973. *Mahopādhyāya's Jaina Tarka Bhāṣā, With Translation and Critical Notes*. Delhi: Motilal Banarsidas.

Bhatt, Govardhan P., 1989: *The Basic Ways of Knowing. An In-depth Study of Kumārila's Contribution to Indian Epistemology*. Delhi, etc.: Motilal Banarsidass.

Bhattacharya, Hari Mohan, 1994. *Jaina Logic and Epistemology*. Calcutta and New Delhi: K. P. Bagchi and Co.

Daly, Chris and David Liggins, 2010: "In defence of error theory". *Philosophical Studies* 149: 209–230. DOI 10.1007/ s11098-009-9346-1.

Dasgupta, Surendranath, 1952: *A History of Indian Philosophy*. Vol. 2. Cambridge: Cambridge University Press.

Datta, D. M., 1960: *The Six Ways of Knowing. A Critical Study of the Vedānta Theory of Knowledge*. Calcutta: University of Calcutta.

Deleu, Jozef,1996: *Viyāhapannatti (Bhagavaī)*, the fifth Aṅga of the Jaina Canon, introduction, critical analysis, commentary and Indexes. Delhi: Motilal Banarsidass.

Dixit, K. K., 1971: *Jaina Ontology*, Ahmedabad: L. D. Institute of Indology.

——— 1974 tr.): *Pt. Sukhlalji's Commentary on Tattvārtha Sāttra of Vācaka Umāsvāti*, Ahmedabad: L. D. Institute of Indology, 1974 (the original Gujarati version was published in 1930 and in Hindi in 1939).

Dundas, Paul, 2002: *The Jains*. London, etc.: Routledge, second ed, (first published 1992).

Duquette, Jonathan and K. Ramasubramanian: "*Anyathākhyāti*: A Critique by Appaya Dīkṣita in the *Parimala*" in *Journal of Indian Philosophy*, January 2009, volume 37: 331–347.

Frauwallner, Erich, 1958: "Die Erkenntnislehre des klassischen Sāṃkhya-Systems" in *Winer Zeitschrift für die Kunde Süd- und Ostasiens*, Vol. II, pp. 85–139 (= *Erich Frauwallner Kleine Schriften*, Wiesbaden: Franz Steiner Verlag, 1982, pp. 223–278).

——— 1984. *Erich Frauwallner: Nachgelassene Werke I: Aufsatze, Beitrage, Skizzen*, Wien: Osterreichische Akademie der Wissenschaften. (Translated from the German in Soni 1994.)

——— 1994: Tr. from the German by J. Soni: *Erich Frauwallner's Posthumous Essays*, Delhi: Aditya Prakashan, 1994. German title: *Erich Frauwallner: Nachgelassene Werke I: Aufsätze, Beiträge, Skizzen*, Wien: Österreichische Akademie der Wissenschaften, 1984.

Fujinaga, Sin, 1999: "Samantabhadra's Epistemology: Combining Jaina Ideas with the Ideas of Other Schools". In Wagle and Qvarnström, pp. 131—137.

Ganeri, Jonardon, 2008: "Worlds in Conflict. The Cosmopolitan Vision of Yaśovijaya Gaṇi". *International Journal of Jaina Studies (Online)*, Vol. 4, No. 1, pp. 1–11. (Accessed 28th October 2015.)

Ghoshal, Saratchandra, 2002: *Āpta-Mīmāṁsā of Āchārya Samantabhadra*. Edited with Introduction, Translation. Notes and An Original Commentary in English. Delhi: Bharatiya Jnanpith. (See also Vidyānandin.)

Hemacandra (eleventh century), 1970. Hemacandra's *Pramāṇa-mīmāṃsā*. Text and translation with critical notes by Satkari Mookerjee. Varanasi: Tara Book Agency. Reprint, 1986.

Hiriyanna, M., 1975: *Indian Conception of Values*. Mysore: Kavyalaya Publishers.

Jacobi, Hermann (tr.), 1895: *Jaina Sūtras*, Part II Sacred Books of the East, Vol. 45, reprinted Delhi: Motilal Banarsidass, 1980.

Jain 1992: see Pūjyapāda 1992.

Jaini, Padmanabh S., 1998: *The Jaina Path of Purification*. Delhi: Motilal Banarsidass.

——— 1978: *Amṛtacandrasūri's Laghutattvasphoṭa*. Edited (and tr.) by Padmanabh S. Jaini. Ahmedabad: L.D. Institute of Indology (L.D. Series 62).

Kundakunda (dates vary from the second to eighth centuries):

1905 ed.: *Pañcāstikāya* (with Amṛtacandra's comm., etc.), Agas (Gujarat): Śrīmad Rājacandra Āśrama. This edition is dated *vikrama saṃvat* 1961. Fifth reprint in 1998 (*vi. saṃ.* 2054).

1931 ed.: *Niyamasāra (The Perfect Law)*, ed. Uggar Sain, Lucknow: The Central Jaina Publishing House. Contains "the original text in Prakrit, with its Samskrit renderings, translation ...."

1975 ed.: *Pañcāstikāyasāra. The Building of the Cosmos*, Prakrit text, Sanskrit chāyā, English commentary, etc.... by Chakravartinayanar with the text, Sanskrit *chāya* and Amṛtacandra's commentary and various readings edited by A. N. Upadhye, Delhi: Bharatiya Jnanpith.

1983 ed. *Pañcāstikāyaḥ*. Agas: Srimad Rajacandra Ashram.

1984 ed.: *Pravacanasāra (Pavayaṇasāra)*, Agās (Gujarat): Śrīmad Rājacandra Āśrama (Prakrit text with the Sanskrit commentaries of

Amṛtacandra and Jayasena, Hindi commentary by Hemarāja). The Prakrit *gāthās* are translated into Sanskrit by Amṛtacandra. The work was edited by A. N. Upadhye who gives an exhaustive introduction in English (pp. 1–126) and also translated the *gāthās* alone into English (pp. 384–410).

Māṇikyanandin (ninth-tenth century), 1940 ed.: *Parīkṣāmukham* by Māṇikyanandī (with *Prameya-ratnamalā* by Anantavīrya). Edited with translation, introduction, notes, and an original commentary in English by Sarat Chandra Ghosal. Lucknow: Central Jaina Publishing House.

Matilal, Bimal Krishna, 1981, *The Central Philosophy of Jainism (Anekānta-vāda)*. Ahmedabad: L.D. Institute of Indology.

Ohira, Suzuko, 1982: *A Study of the Tattvārthasūtra with Bhāṣya with Special Reference to Authorship and Date*. Ahmedabad: L. D. Institute of Indology.

G. Oberhammer, 1960: "The Authorship of the Ṣaṣṭitantram", *Wiener Zeitschrift für die Kunde Süd- und Ostasiens*, Leiden: E. J. Brill, vol. 4, pp. 71–91.

——— 1963: "Ein Beitrag zu den vāda-Traditionen Indiens" *Wiener Zeitschrift für die Kunde Süd- und Ostasiens*, Leiden: E.J. Brill, vol. 7, pp. 63–103.

Padmarajiah, Y. J., 1963: *A Comparative Study of the Jaina Theories of Reality and Knowledge*. Delhi: Motilal Banarsidass. Reprint, 1986.

Paṇṇavaṇāsutta (Prajñāpanāsūtra) in two parts being the fourth *Upāṅga* of the Jaina canon, edited by Muni Puṇyavijaya, Pt. Dalasukha Mālvaṇiā, and Pt Amṛtlāla Mohanalāla Bhojak:

1969: Part 1, Bombay: Śrī Mahāvīra Jaina Vidyālaya (Jaina-Āgama-Series Vol. 9).

1971: Part 2, Bombay: Śrī Mahāvīra Jaina Vidyālaya (Jaina-Āgama-Series Vol. 9), Introduction and Indexes, with the introduction translated by Nagin J. Shah into English from the Gujarātī.

2000 ed.: Ahmedabad: Āgama Ārādhanā Kendra, Parts 10–11, with the commentary (*vṛtti*) by Malayagiri.

PaSā = Kundakunda's *Pañcāstikāyasāra*.

PraSā = Kundakunda's *Pravacanasāra (Pavayaṇasāra)*.

PraSū = *Paṇṇavaṇāsutta (Prajñāpanāsūtra)*.

Potter, Karl H. (general ed.), 2007: *Encyclopedia of Indian Philosophies. Volume X. Jain Philosophy Part I*, edited by Dalsukh Malvania and Jayendra Soni. Delhi: Motilal Banarsidass.

——— 2013: *Encyclopedia of Indian Philosophies. Volume XIV. Jain Philosophy Part II*, edited by Karl H. Potter & Piotr Balcerowicz. Delhi: Motilal Banarsidass.

——— 2014: *Encyclopedia of Indian Philosophies. Volume XVII. Jain Philosophy Part Three*, edited by Piotr Balcerowicz and Karl H. Potter . Delhi: Motilal Banarsidass.

Prasad, Jwala, 1939: *Indian Epistemology*. Lahore: Motilal Banarsidass.

Pūjyapāda (sixth century), 1955 ed.: *Sarvārthasiddhi* [a commentary on Umāsvāti's *Tattvārthasūtra*], Kaśī: Bhāratīya Jñānapīṭha, edited [and translated into Hindī] by Phūlacandra Śāstrī [entails the Digambara version of the TS.]

———1992: *Reality. English Translation of Shri Pujyapada's Sarvartha-siddhi*. Tr. S. A. Jain Madras: Jwalamalini Trust, second edition [actually a reprint of the first edition published in Calcutta: Vira Sasana Sangha, 1960].

Randle, H. N., 1930/1937: *Indian Logic in the Early Schools: A Study of the Nyāya-darśana in Its Relation to the Early Logic of Other Schools*. Oxford: Oxford University Press. Reprint, Delhi: Munshiram Manoharlal.

Rao, Srinivasa, 1998: *Perceptual Error. The Indian Theories*. Honolulu: University of Hawa'i Press.

Ruegg D. Seyfort, 1962–62: "Note on Vārṣagaṇya and the *Yogācāra-bhūmi*" *Indo-Iranian Journal*, Hague: Mouton and Co. vol. 6, pp. 137–140.

Ṣaṭkaṇḍāgama by Puṣpadanta and Bhātabali, with the commentary *Dhavalā* by Vīrasena, in 16 volumes, Solapur: Jaina Samskriti Samrakshaka Sangha, third revised ed. 1992.

Shah 1971: see *Paṇṇavaṇāsutta (Prajñāpanāsūtra)* 1971.

Shah, Nagin J. (ed.), 2002: *Hemacandra's Pramāṇamīmāṃsā. A Critiques of Organ of Knowledge. A work on Jaina Logic*. Ahmedabad: Gujarat Vidyapith (International Centre for Jaina Studies).

Shastri, Indra Chandra:, 1990: *Jaina Epistemology*, Varanasi: P. V. Research Institute.

Soni, Jayandra, 1989: *Philosophical Anthropology in Śaiva Siddhānta. With special reference to Śivāgrayogin*. Delhi: Motilal Banarsidass Publishers (to be republished by 2017).

——— 1991: "*Dravya, Guṇa* and *Paryāya* in Jaina Thought" in *Journal of Indian Philosophy*, Netherlands: Kluwer, Vol. 19, 1991 pp. 75–88.

——— 1996a: *Aspects of Jaina Philosophy*. Three lectures on Jainism published on behalf of the University of Madras, Department of Jainism, by the Research Foundation for Jainology, Madras. Annual Lecture Series 1994–95. Contents: The Karma Theory and Jaina Ethics; *Syādvāda* is not *Samśayavāda*; and Vidyānandin on Umāsvāti's *pramāṇa-nayair adhigamaḥ*, (*Tattvārthasūtra* 1, 6), 60 pp.

——— 1996b: *The Notion of Āpta in Jaina Philosophy*, the 1995 Roop Lal Jain Annual Lecture, Toronto, 25 November 1995.Toronto: University of Toronto, Centre for South Asia Studies, 20 pp.

——— 1998: Three articles on Jaina Philosophy in Edward Craig (ed.): *Routledge Encyclopaedia of Philosophy*. The titles are: 'Mahāvīra' (1000 words); 'Manifoldness, Jaina Theory of (*Anekāntavāda*)' (3000 words); 'Jaina Philosophy, Issues in' (6000 words).

——— 1999a: "Aspects of Jaina Epistemology with Special Reference to Vidyānandin". Paper presented at the conference 'Approaches to Jain Studies', Toronto March 31–April 2, 1995. Published in *Approaches to Jain Studies: Philosophy, Logic, Rituals and Symbols*. Toronto: University of Toronto, Centre for South Asian Studies, in the series South Asian Papers, no. 11, pp. 138–168.

——— 1999b: "Mahāvīra" (approx. 1000 words) in "The Blackwell Companions to Philosophy". *A Companion to the Philosophers*, ed. Robert L. Arrington, pp. 595–597.

——— 2000: "Basic Jaina Epistemology" in *Philosophy East and West*, Vol. 50, No. 3. pp. 367–377.

——— 2001a: edited *Vasantagauravam. Essays in Jainism. Felicitating Professor M. D. Vasantha Raj of Mysore on the Occasion of his Seventy-Fifth Birthday*. Mumbai: Vakils, Feffer and Simons Ltd. Article in it: "A Note on the Jaina *tattva/padārtha*", pp. 135–140.

——— 2001b: *Trustworthiness. Universals and Particulars. Two Essays in Jaina Philosophy* (75 page booklet). Ed. S. P. Patil, Dhawad: Karnatak University.

——— 2002: Epistemological Categories in the "*Akalaṅkagranthatrayam*" in Dragomir Dimitrov et al. (eds): *Śikhisamuccayaḥ, Indian and Tibetan Studies*, Wien: Arbeitskreis für tibetische und buddhistische Studien Universität Wien, pp. 185–191.

——— 2003a: "Kundakunda and Umāsvāti on *Anekāntavāda*" in Piotr Balcerowicz (ed.): *Caturaranayacakram. Essays in Jaina Philosophy and Religion*. Warsaw Indological Studies (ed. P. Balcerowicz and M. Mejor) Volume 2, 2002, pp. 25–35. Printed in Delhi: Motilal Banarsidass (Lala Sundarlal Jain Research Series, general editor: Professor Satya Ranjan Banerjee). Proceedings of the international seminar 'Aspects of Jainism' at the University of Warsaw, Poland, 8–9 September 2000.

——— 2003b: "On the Origin and Development of Epistemology in Indian Philosophy" in *Polylog*, 4, 2003. Also online: http://them.polylog.org/4/ fsj-en.htm.

——— 2007a: "*Anekāntavāda* Revisited—for doṣas" in *Indica et Tibetica. Festschrift für Michael Hahn zum 65. Geburtstag*, Wien: Arbeitskreis

für tibetische und buddhistische Studien, Universitaet Wien, pp. 477–490.
——— 2007b: "*Upayoga*, according to Kundakunda and Umāsvāti" in *Journal of Indian Philosophy*, 2007, 35: 299–311.
——— 2007c: Edited together with Dalsukh Malvania: *Encyclopedia of Indian Philosophies Volume X. Jain Philosophy (Part I)*. Articles: "Introduction", pp. 3–34 and "Devasena, *Tattvasāra* Summary", pp. 527–532.
——— 2009: "A Section of Vidyānandin's Critique of Buddhism" in *Pāsādikadānaṁ. Fesctschrift für Bhikkhu Pāsādika*, ed. Straube, et al. Marburg: Indica et Tibetica Verlag, pp. 449–458.
——— 2012, Edited: *Jaina Studies. Proceedings of the DOT 2010 Panel in Marburg, Germany*, ed. by Jayandra Soni. New Delhi: Aditya Prakashan. Contributions: "Introduction", pp. 1–5 and "Jaina Epistemology Revisited: On Erroneous Cognition", pp. 97–112.
——— 2013: "Prabhācandra's Status in and Contribution to the History of Jaina Philosophical Speculation", paper presented at the 15th Jaina Studies Workshop, SOAS (School of Oriental and African Studies), London. Published online here:
http://www.soas.ac.uk/research/publications/journals/ijjs/file88721.pdf.
——— 2015a: edited with Luitgard Soni: *Sanmati. Essays in Honour of Professor Hampa Nagarajaiah*. Bengaluru Sapna Book House. Article: "A Sketch of Jaina Epistemology", pp. 377–382.
——— 2015b: "Aspects of Philosophy in the *Ṣaṭkhaṇḍāgama*". In Peter Flügel and Olle Qvarnström (eds): *Jaina Scriptures and Philosophy*. London/New York: Routledge, pp. 133–144.
——— 2016: "Yoga in the *Tattvārthasūtra*". In Christopher Key Chapple (ed.): *Yoga in Jainism*. London/New York: Routledge, pp. 29–36.
——— 2017: "Jaina Virtue Ethics: Action and Nonaction" in: *The Bloomsbury Research Handbook of Indian Ethics*, edited by Shyam Ranganathan, Bloomsbury, London, etc., pp. 155–176.
——— forthcoming 2018: Section editor of 'Jaina Logic' in: *Indian Logic* edited by Sundar Sarukkai, London, etc.: Springer. Article: "A General Introduction to Logic in Jainism with a List of Logicians and their Texts". The submitted version is in over 7000 words.
SS = *Sarvārthasiddhi*, see Pūjyapāda.
Tatia, Nathmal, 1951: *Studies in Jaina Philosophy*, Varanasi: P. V. Research Institute.
——— 1994: *Tattvārthasūtra. That Which Is. Umāsvāti/Umāsvāmī with the combined commentaries of Umāsvāti/Umāsvāmī, Pūjyapāda and*

Siddhasenagaṇi. Translated with an introduction. San Francisco, etc.: HarperCollins Publishers.

Trikha, Himal, 2012: *Perspektivismus und Kritik. Das pluralistische Erkenntnismodell der Jainas angesichts der Polemik gegen das Vaiśeṣika in Vidyānandins Satyaśāsanaparīkṣā*. Publications of the De Nobili Research Library edited by Gerhard Oberhammer, Utz Podzeit and Karin Preisendanz, Volume XXXVI. Wien: Sammlung de Nobili ... Universität.

——— 2015: "Trends of Research on Philosophical Sanskrit Works of the Jainas" in Luitgard Soni and Jayandra Soni (eds): *Sanmati. Essays Felicitating Professor Hampa Nagarajaiah on the Occasion of his 80th Birthday*. Bengaluru: Sapna Book House.

TS = *Tattvārthasūtra* of Umāsvāti, also called *Tattvārtādhigamasūtra*. See Pūjyapāda 1955 ed. for the Digambara version of the TS, and Umāsvāti 1932 ed. for the Śvetāmbara version of the TS, quoted here where necessary with a slash (/) giving the Digambara version first). See also Tatia 1994.

Umāsvāti (*c.* fifth century), 1932 ed.: *Sabhāṣyatattvārthādhigamasūtra*, Bambaī: Maṇīlāla, Revāśaṃkara Jagajivana Jhaverī.

Upadhye, A.N., 1971: *Siddhasena Divākara's Nyāyāvatāra ... as well as the Text of 21 Dvātriṁśikās and the Sammaï-Suttam*. Bombay: Jaina Sāhitya Vikāsa Maṇḍala.

Upadhye 1984: see Kundakunda 1984 ed.: *Pravacanasāra (Pavayaṇa-sāra)*.

Vidyabhusana, Satis Chandra, 1971: *A History of Indian Logic (Ancient, Mediaeval and Modern Schools.)*. Delhi: Motilal Banarsidass (Jaina Logic pp. 157–224).

Vidyānandin (*c.* ninth c. also called Vidyānanda), 1918 ed.: *Tattvārtha-ślokavārtikam*, ed. Paṇḍita Manoharalāla, Bombay: Nirnaya Sagar Press.

Wiley, Kristi L., 2004: *Historical Dictionary of Jainism*. Lanham, etc.: The Scarecrow Press.

Index